John Stockdale, Thomas Erskine

The whole Proceedings on the Trial of an Information Exhibited Ex Officio

John Stockdale, Thomas Erskine

The whole Proceedings on the Trial of an Information Exhibited Ex Officio

ISBN/EAN: 9783337399023

Printed in Europe, USA, Canada, Australia, Japan

Cover: Foto ©Suzi / pixelio.de

More available books at **www.hansebooks.com**

THE WHOLE PROCEEDINGS

·ON THE

T R I A L

OF AN INFORMATION EXHIBITED EX OFFICIO,
BY THE KING'S ATTORNEY GENERAL,

AGAINST

JOHN STOCKDALE;

FOR

A LIBEL ON THE HOUSE OF COMMONS,

TRIED IN THE COURT OF KING'S-BENCH WEST-
MINSTER, ON WEDNESDAY, THE NINTH OF
DECEMBER, 1789,

BEFORE THE RIGHT HON. LLOYD LORD
KENYON, CHIEF JUSTICE OF ENGLAND.

———

TAKEN IN SHORT HAND BY

JOSEPH GUR·NEY.

———

TO WHICH IS SUBJOINED,

AN ARGUMENT

IN SUPPORT OF

THE RIGHTS OF JURIES.

L O N D O N:
PRINTED FOR JOHN STOCKDALE, OPPOSITE BURLINGTON-
HOUSE, PICCADILLY.
M,DCC,XC.
[Entered at Stationers-Hall.]

CONTENTS.

PREFACE.

THE Pamphlet which gave rife to the following Trial, was written by the Reverend Mr. Logan, fome time one of the miniſters of Leith, near Edinburgh;—"A gentleman formed to be the ornament and inſtructor of the age in which he lived : All his writings are diſtinguiſhed by the fagacity of their reaſonings, the brilliancy of their imaginations, and the depth of their philoſophical principles. Though cut off in the flower of his age, while the proſecution

A 3   againſt

againft his publifher was depending, he left behind him feveral refpectable productions, and particularly Elements of Lectures upon the Philofophy of Ancient Hiftory; which, though imperfect, and unfinifhed' will afford to the difcerning, fufficient reafon to regret that his talents did not remain to be matured by age, and expanded by the foftering breath of public applaufe."

Such is the character, given of Mr. Logan in the laft New Annual Regifter; but as his Review of the Charges againft Mr. Haftings has made fo much noife in the world, it may not be uninterefting to ftate by what means, he became fo intimately acquainted, with the politics of India.

For fome time previous to his deceafe, Mr. Logan was the principal author of that part of the Englifh Review, which gives the general ftate of foreign and domeftic

tic politics. The enquiries in the Houſe of
Commons, which led to the impeachment
of Mr. Haſtings, formed very naturally the
moſt material part of that Review for a
conſiderable time ; and his Strictures upon
the arguments, and the deciſion on the
Benares and the Begum charges, are written
with great force and elegance; and contain reflections infinitely more pointed, than
any of thoſe which Mr. Fox objected to in
his pamphlet.

Having qualified himſelf by the information that he had acquired, from intenſe
application, to give to the world what he
conceived to be a fair and impartial account of the adminiſtration of Mr. Haſtings,
he ſat down voluntarily, without a wiſh or
proſpect of perſonal advantage, to examine
thoſe articles which had been preſented to the
Houſe of Commons by the Managers, then
a Committee of Secreſy, and which now form

the

the articles before the Lords. When he had compleated his pamphlet, he fubmitted it in manufcript to the perufal of a gentleman, who is intimately connected with Mr. Haftings. That gentleman was certainly very ill qualified to advife him, as a lawyer; it never having entered into his imagination, that after the torrent of abufe that had been poured out upon Mr. Haftings, for years, *any thing* faid in reply could be deemed libellous, and therefore he merely examined whether Mr. Logan was correct in his ftatement of facts, and communicated to him every particular relative to the laft thirteen articles. Not fatisfied with this communication, Mr. Logan examined the votes and the fpeeches, as printed and circulated throughout Great Britain. After an accurate inveftigation, he thought himfelf juftified in inferting in his pamphlet, what a member had faid in the Houfe, that the

Commons

Commons had voted thirteen out of twenty articles, without reading them.

The bookseller to whom Mr. Logan originally presented his pamphlet, offered a sum for it, which he conceived so inadequate to its importance, that he carried it to Mr. Stockdale, to whom he gave it; taking for himself a few copies only, which were sent in his name to men of the first eminence in letters, both in London and Edinburgh.

After it had been some time in circulation, and read with great avidity, it was publicly complained of by Mr. Fox. That gentleman quoted what he conceived to be the libellous passages. The following day he moved an address to his Majesty, to direct his Attorney General to prosecute the authors and publishers, and the motion was carried *nemine contradicente;* but owing to the sickness of the principal witness, the trial was deferred for nearly two years. This prosecution which

has

has been attended with a very heavy expence to Mr. Stockdale, and has been
nearly two years depending, hath excited
univerſal attention.

The acknowledged accuracy of Mr. Gur-
ney, is too well known to require any particular praiſe on this occaſion; but it never
was more remarkable than in the preſent inſtance; yet the eloquent and excellent
ſpeech of Mr. Erſkine, will appear to great
diſadvantage to thoſe who had the good fortune to hear it, ſo much, even the beſt ſpeeches
depend upon the power of delivery. It was
ſpoke in as crowded a Court, as ever appeared in the King's-Bench. The exertions of that gentleman in ſupport of his
clients are too well known, to acquire new
force from any thing that can be ſaid of
him here ; but on no occaſion, and at no
period, did he diſplay thoſe wonderful abilities that he poſſeſſes in a higher degree,
and Mr. Erſkine will be quoted as the ſteady
friend,

friend, and fupporter of the Conftitutional Rights of the people of Great-Britain, as long as the facred flame of Liberty fhall animate the breaft of an Englifhman,

The refult of this Trial proves how dangerous to public liberty it would be, were any body of men, parties and judges in their own caufe. No good fubject will call into queftion unneceffarily, any of the privileges claimed by the Houfe of Commons; but if in the inftance before us, the Houfe, confulting former precedents, had taken upon itfelf to ftate the crime, and to pronounce judgment, a Britifh fubject might have been feized and imprifoned fome months, probably to the ruin of himfelf and his family, without the poffibility of reparation. It may therefore with the greateft truth be obferved, that by the exertions of Mr. Erfkine, and by the decifion on this profecution, the Freedom of the Prefs, and the Liberty of the Subject, are fully fecured,

January 13*th*, 1790.

ERRATA.

Page 38 Line 19, for conteſt, read context.
——— 49 ——— 18, for Loggan, read Logan.
——— 50 ——— 6, for policys, read policies.
——— 56 ——— for ſupport, read ſuppoſed.
——— 65 ——— 12, and 17, for Lord Cornwallis, read
                    Sir J. Maopherſon.
——— 115 ——— 21, for bais, read bias.

THE

TRIAL

OF

JOHN STOCKDALE.

THE INFORMATION.

Of Easter Term, *in the Twenty-eighth Year of the Reign of King* George *the Third.*

Middlesex,
to wit. }
BE it remembered, That Richard Pepper Arden, Esquire, Attorney General of our present Sovereign Lord the King, who for our present Sovereign Lord the King in this behalf prosecuteth, in his own proper person comes here into the Court of our said Lord the King, before the King himself, at Westminster, on Wednesday next after fifteen days from the feast day of Easter in this same term, and for our said Lord the King giveth the Court here to

B   understand

underſtand and be informed, that before the printing and publiſhing of the ſeveral falſe, ſcandalous, infamous, wicked, malicious, and ſeditious libels, herein after mentioned, the Commons of Great Britain in Parliament aſſembled, had, at the bar of the Houſe of Lords, impeached Warren Haſtings, Eſquire, late Governor General of Bengal, of high crimes and miſdemeanors, and had there exhibited divers articles of impeachment of high crimes and miſdemeanors againſt the ſaid Warren Haſtings, to wit, at Weſtminſter aforeſaid, in the county of Middleſex aforeſaid; yet John Stockdale, late of the pariſh of St. James's, Weſtminſter, in the county of Middleſex, Bookſeller, well knowing the premiſes, but being a wicked, ſeditious, and ill-diſpoſed perſon, and having no regard for the laws of this realm, or for the public peace and tranquillity of this kingdom, and moſt unlawfully, wickedly, and maliciouſly deviſing, contriving, and intending to aſperſe, ſcandalize, and vilify the Commons of Great Britain in Parliament aſſembled, and moſt wickedly and audaciouſly to repreſent their proceedings in Parliament as corrupt and unjuſt, and to make it to be believed and thought as if the majority of the Commons of Great Britain in Parliament aſſembled, were a moſt wicked, tyrannical, baſe, and corrupt ſet of perſons, and to bring the Commons of Great Britain in Parliament aſſembled into hatred and contempt with the ſubjects of this kingdom, and to raiſe,

excite,

excite, and create moſt groundleſs diſtruſts in the minds of all the King's ſubjects, as if from the profligacy and wickedneſs of the Commons of Great Britain in Parliament aſſembled, great injuſtice would be done to the ſaid Warren Haſtings on the fifteenth day of February, in the twenty-eighth year of the reign of our ſaid preſent Sovereign Lord the King, at Weſtminſter afore-ſaid, in the county of Middleſex aforeſaid; with force and arms, unlawfully, wickedly, maliciouſly, and ſeditiouſly printed and publiſhed, and cauſed and procured to be printed and publiſhed, in a certain book, or pamphlet, intitled,

" A Review of the Principal Charges againſt
" Warren Haſtings, Eſquire, late Go-
" vernor General of Bengal,"

A certain falſe, ſcandalous, wicked, ſeditious, and malicious libel of and concerning the ſaid impeachment of the ſaid Warren Haſtings, ſo exhibited as aforeſaid, and of and concerning the Commons of Great Britain in Parliament aſſembled, containing amongſt other things divers falſe, ſcandalous, ſeditious, and malicious matters of and concerning the ſaid impeachment, and of and concerning the Commons of Great Britain in Parliament aſſembled, according to the tenor and effect following (to wit): The Houſe of Commons (meaning the Commons of Great

Britain

Britain in Parliament affembled,) has now given
its final decifion with regard to the merits and
demerits of Mr. Haftings, (meaning the faid
Warren Haftings, Efquire, late Governor General
of Bengal.) The grand inqueft of England,
(meaning the faid Commons of Great Britain
in Parliament affembled,) have delivered their
charges (meaning the charges of the faid
Commons of Great Britain in Parliament
affembled,) and preferred their impeachment
(meaning their impeachment of the faid Warren
Haftings,); their allegations are referred to proof,
and from the appeal to the collective wifdom and
juftice of the nation, in the fupreme tribunal of
the kingdom, (meaning the Lords Spiritual and
Temporal in Parliament affembled,) the queftion
comes to be determined, Whether Mr. Haftings (meaning the faid Warren Haftings, Efquire,)
be guilty or not guilty? What credit can we give
to multiplied and accumulated charges, (meaning
the faid charges of high crimes and mifdemeanors
fo exhibited, by the Commons of Great Britain
in Parliament affembled as aforefaid, againft the faid
Warren Haftings,) when we find that they (meaning
the faid charges of high crimes and mifdemeanors
fo exhibited by the Commons of Great Britain in
Parliament affembled as aforefaid, againft the faid
Warren Haftings) originate from mifreprefentation
and falfehood, (meaning thereby to caufe it to be
believed and underftood, that the faid charges
of high crimes and mifdemeanors fo exhibited by
the

the Commons of Great Britain in Parliament affembled as aforefaid, did originate from mifreprefentation and falfehood,); and in another part thereof according to the tenor and effect following (to wit): An impeachment of error in judgment, with regard to the quantum of a fine, and for an intention that never was executed and never known to the offending party, characterifes a tribunal inquifition rather than a Court of Parliament (meaning thereby to caufe it to be believed and underftood that the Commons of Great Britain in Parliament affembled had proceeded in the faid impeachment of the faid Warren Haftings in a manner unjuft and unworthy of a Houfe of Parliament of Great Britain,); and in another part thereof, according to the tenor and effect following (to wit): The other charges (meaning divers of the charges of the faid impeachment againft the faid Warren Haftings, Efquire) are fo infignificant in themfelves, or founded on fuch grofs mifreprefentations, that they would not affect an obfcure individual, much lefs a public character; they are merely added to fwell the catalogue of accufations, as if the boldnefs of calumny would infure its fuccefs, and a multiplicity of charges were an accumulation of crimes. Thirteen of them (meaning thirteen of the faid charges fo exhibited by the Commons of Great Britain in Parliament affembled againft the faid Warren Haftings, Efquire, as aforefaid) paffed in the Houfe of Commons (meaning the faid Commons of Great

Britain

Britain in Parliament affembled) not only without inveftigation, but without being read; and the votes (meaning the votes of the Commons of Great Britain in Parliament affembled) were given without enquiry, argument, or conviction; a majority (meaning a majority of the Commons of Great Britain in Parliament affembled) had determined to impeach; oppofite parties met each other and juftled in the dark, to perplex the political drama and bring the hero (meaning the faid Warren Haftings, Efquire,) to a tragic cataftrophe; and in another part thereof, according to the tenor and effect following (to wit): But if, after exerting all your efforts in the caufe of your country, you return covered with laurels and crowned with fuccefs, if you preferve a loyal attachment to your Sovereign you may expect the thunders of parliamentary vengeance; you will certainly be impeached, and probably be undone (meaning thereby to caufe it to be believed and underftood, that the Commons of Great Britain in Parliament affembled had impeached the faid Warren Haftings of high crimes and mifdemeanors, not from motives of juftice, but becaufe the faid Warren Haftings had exerted all his efforts in the caufe of his country, and returned covered with laurels and crowned with fuccefs, and preferved a loyal attachment to our faid prefent Sovereign Lord the King); and in another part thereof, according to the tenor and effect following (to wit): The office of calm deliberate
juftice

juftice is to redrefs grievances as well as to punifh offences. It has been affirmed; that the natives of India have been deeply injured; but has any motion been made to make them compenfation for the injuries they have fuftained? Have the accufers of Mr. Haftings (meaning the faid Warren Haftings, Efquire,) ever propofed to bring back the Rohillas to the country from which they were expelled? to reftore Cheit Sing to the Zemindary of Benares? or to return to the Nabob of Oude, the prefent which the Governor of Bengal received from him, for the benefit of the Company? till fuch meafures are adopted, and in the train of negociation, the world has every reafon to conclude that the impeachment of Mr. Haftings (meaning the faid impeachment fo exhibited by the faid Commons of Great Britain in Parliament affembled, againft the faid Warren Haftings, Efquire, is carried on from motives of perfonal animofity, not from regard to public juftice, to the great fcandal and difhonour of the Commons of Great Britain in Parliament affembled, and in high contempt of their authority, to the great difturbance of the public peace and tranquillity of this kingdom, in contempt of our prefent Sovereign Lord the King and his laws, to the evil and pernicious example of all others in the like cafe offending, and alfo againft the peace of our faid Sovereign Lord the King, his crown and dignity. And the faid Attorney General of our faid

prefent

prefent Lord the King, for our faid Lord the
King, further giveth the Court here to underftand
and be informed, that the faid John Stockdale,
being fuch perfon as aforefaid, and contriving, and
wickedly and malicioufly devifing and intending
as aforefaid, afterwards, to wit, on the fifteenth day
of February, in the twenty-eighth year aforefaid,
at Weftminfter aforefaid, in the county aforefaid,
with force and arms, unlawfully, wickedly, malicioufly and feditioufly printed and publifhed, and
caufed to be printed and publifhed, in a certain
other book, or pamphlet, intitled,

" A Review of the Principal Charges againft
" Warren Haftings, Efquire, late Gover-
" nor General of Bengal,"

A certain other falfe, fcandalous, wicked, feditious,
and malicious libel, of and concerning the faid
impeachment of the faid Warren Haftings, fo
exhibited as aforefaid, and of and concerning the
Commons of Great Britain in Parliament affembled, containing, amongft other things, according
to the tenor and effect following (to wit.) What
credit can we give to the multiplied and accumulated charges (meaning the faid charges of high
crimes and mifdemeanors, fo exhibited by the
Commons of Great Britain in Paliament affembled
as aforefaid, againft the faid Warren Haftings,)
when

when we find that they (meaning the said charges
of high crimes and misdemeanors, so exhibited by
the Commons of Great Britain in Parliament af-
sembled as aforesaid, against the said Warren
Haftings,) originate from misreprefentation and
falsehood (meaning thereby to caufe it to be
believed and underftood, that the said charges of
high crimes and misdemeanors, so exhibited by
the Commons of Great Britain, in Parliament
affembled as aforesaid, did originate from misreprefentation and falsehood, to the great scandal
and dishonour of the Commons of Great Britain
in Parliament affembled, and in high contempt of
their authority; to the great disturbance of the
public peace and tranquillity of this kingdom; in
contempt of our prefent Sovereign Lord the King
and his laws, to the evil and pernicious example
of all others in the like cafe offending; and alfo,
againft the peace of our said prefent Sovereign
Lord the King, his crown and dignity. And the
said Attorney General of our said Lord the King,
for our said Lord the King, further gives the Court
here to underftand and be informed, that the said
John Stockdale, being fuch perfon as aforesaid, and
contriving and wickedly and malicioufly devifing
and intending as aforesaid, afterwards, to wit, on
the fifteenth day of February, in the twenty-eighth
year aforesaid, at Weftminfter aforesaid, in the
county aforesaid, with force and arms, unlawfully,
wickedly, malicioufly and feditioufly printed and
publifhed, and caufed to be printed and publifhed,

lifhed, in a certain other book, or pamplet, intitled,

" A Review of the Principal Charges againft
" Warren Haftings, Efquire, late Gover-
" nor General of Bengal,"

A certain other falfe, fcandalous, wicked, feditious, and malicious libel, of and concerning the faid impeachment of the faid Warren
Haftings, fo exhibited as aforefaid, and of and
concerning the Commons of Great Britain
in Parliament affembled, containing, amongft
other things, according to the tenor and effect
following (to wit): An impeachment of error
in judgment, with regard to the quantum of
a fine, and for an intention that never was
executed, and never known to the offending party,
characterifes a tribunal inquifition, rather than a
Court of Parliament; (meaning thereby to caufe
it to be believed and underftood, that the Commons of Great Britain in Parliament affembled,
had proceeded in the faid impeachment of the faid
Warren Haftings, in a manner unjuft, and unworthy of a Houfe of Parliament of Great Britain):
to the great fcandal and difhonour of the Commons of Great Britain in Parliament affembled,
and in high contempt of their authority; to the
great difturbance of the public peace and tranquillity
of this kingdom ; in contempt of our faid prefent
Sovereign

Sovereign Lord the King and his laws, to the evil
and pernicious example of all others in the like
cafe offending; and alfo, againft the peace of our faid
prefent Sovereign Lord the King, his crown and
dignity, &c.   And the faid Attorney General
of our faid Lord the King, for our faid Lord the
King, further gives the court here to underftand,
and be informed, that the faid John Stockdale,
being fuch perfon as aforefaid, and contriving
and wickedly and malicioufly devifing and intending as aforefaid, afterwards, to wit, on the faid fifteenth day of February,   in the   twenty-eighth
year aforefaid,   at Weftminfter aforefaid, in the
county aforefaid, with force and arms, unlawfully,   wickedly,   malicioufly,   and feditioufly,
printed and publifhed, and caufed to be printed
and publifhed, in a certain other book, or pamphlet, intitled,

" A Review of the Principal Charges againft
   " Warren Haftings, Efquire, late Gover-
   " nor General of Bengal,"

A certain other falfe, fcandalous, wicked, feditious,
and malicious libel, of and concerning the faid impeachment of the faid Warren Haftings, fo exhibited as aforefaid, and of and concerning the
Commons of Great Britain in Parliament affembled, containing, amongft other things, according
to the tenor and effect following (to wit):   The
other charges (meaning divers of the charges of
the

the said impeachment againſt the ſaid Warren
Haſtings, Eſquire,) are ſo inſignificant in themſelves, or founded on ſuch groſs miſrepreſenta-
tions, that they would not affect an obſcure individual, much leſs a public character; they are
merely added to ſwell the catalogue of accuſations;
as if the boldneſs of calumny could enſure its ſuc-
ceſs, and a multiplicity of charges were an accumulation of crimes; thirteen of them (meaning
thirteen of the ſaid charges ſo exhibited by the
Commons of Great Britain in Parliament aſſembled, againſt the ſaid Warren Haſtings, Eſquire, as
aforeſaid) paſſed in the Houſe of Commons, (meaning the Commons of Great Britain in Parliament
aſſembled) not only without inveſtigation, but
without being read, and the votes (meaning the
votes of the Commons of Great Britain in Parliament aſſembled) were given without enquiry,
argument, or conviction : a majority (meaning a
majority of the Commons of Great Britain in
Parliament aſſembled) had determined to impeach ;
oppoſite parties met each other and juſtled in the
dark, to perplex the political drama, and bring
the hero (meaning the ſaid Warren Haſtings,
Eſquire,) to a tragic cataſtrophe; to the great
ſcandal and diſhonour of the Commons of Great
Britain in Parliament aſſembled, and in high contempt of their authority; to the great diſturbance
of the public peace and tranquillity of this kingdom; in contempt of our preſent Sovereign Lord
the King and his laws ; to the evil and pernicious
example of all others in the like caſe offending, and
also

alfo againft the peace of our faid prefent Sovereign
Lord the King, his crown and dignity, &c. And
the faid Attorney General of our faid Lord the
King, for our faid Lord the King, further gives
the court here to underftand and be informed,
that the faid John Stockdale, being fuch perfon as
aforefaid, and contriving and wickedly and
malicioufly devifing and intending as aforefaid,
afterwards, to wit, on the faid fifteenth day of
February, in the twenty-eighth year aforefaid, at
Weftminfter aforefaid, in the county aforefaid,
with force and arms, unlawfully, wickedly, malicioufly, and feditioufly, printed and publifhed,
and caufed and procured to be printed and publifhed, in a certain other book, or pamphlet,
intitled,

" A Review of the Principal Charges againft
  " Warren Haftings, Efquire, late Gover-
  " nor General of Bengal,"

A certain other falfe, fcandalous, wicked, feditious, and malicious libel, of and concerning
the faid impeachment of the faid Warren Haftings, fo exhibited as aforefaid, and of and
concerning the Commons of Great Britain in
Parliament affembled, containing, amongft other
things, according to the tenor and effect following
(to wit) : But if after exerting all your efforts in
the caufe of your country, you return covered with
laurels,

laurels, and crowned with fuccefs; if you preferve
a loyal attachment to your Sovereign, you may
expect the thunders of parliamentary vengeance;
you will certainly be impeached, and probably be
undone (meaning thereby to caufe it to be
believed and underftood, that the Commons of
Great Britain in Parliament affembled, had impeached the faid Warren Haftings of high crimes
and mifdemeanors, not from motives of juftice,
but becaufe the faid Warren Haftings had exerted
all his efforts in the caufe of his country, and
returned covered with laurels and crowned with fuccefs, and preferved a loyal attachment to our Sovereign Lord the prefent King); to the great fcandal
and difhonour of the Commons of Great Britain
in Parliament affembled, and in high contempt of
their authority; to the great difturbance of the
public peace and tranquillity of this kingdom; in
contempt of our prefent Sovereign Lord the King,
and his laws; to the pernicious example of all
others in the like cafe offending; and alfo, againft
the peace of our faid prefent Sovereign Lord the
King, his crown and dignity, &c. And the faid
Attorney General of our faid Lord the King, for
our faid Lord the King, further gives the court
here to underftand and be informed, that the faid
John Stockdale, being fuch perfon as aforefaid,
and contriving, and wickedly and malicioufly devifing and intending as aforefaid, afterwards, to
wit, on the faid fifteenth day of February, in the
twenty-eighth year aforefaid, at Weftminfter
aforefaid,

aforefaid, in the county aforefaid, with force and arms, unlawfully, wickedly, malicioufly, and feditioufly printed and publifhed, and caufed and procured to be printed and publifhed, in a certain other book, or pamphlet, intitled,

" A Review of the Principal Charges againft
" Warren Haftings, Efquire, late Gover-
" nor General of Bengal,"

A certain other falfe, fcandalous, wicked, feditious, and malicious libel, of and concerning the faid impeachment of the faid Warren Haftings, fo exhibited as aforefaid, and of and concerning the Commons of Great Britain in Parliament affembled, containing, amongft other things, according to the tenor and effect following (to wit): The office of calm deliberate juftice, is to redrefs grievances as well as to punifh offences. It has been affirmed that the natives of India have been deeply injured, but has any motion been made to make them compenfation for the injuries they have fuftained? have the accufers of Mr. Haftings, (meaning the faid Warren Haftings, Efquire,) ever propofed to bring back the Rohillas to the country from which they were expelled? to reftore Cheit Sing to the Zemindary of Benares? or to return to the Nabob of Oude the prefent, which the Governor of Bengal received from him for the benefit of the Company? till fuch meafures are

adopted,

adopted, and in the train of negociation, the world has every reason to conclude that the impeachment of Mr. Haftings, (meaning the faid impeachment fo exhibited by the Commons of Great Britain in Parliament affembled, againft the faid Warren Haftings, Efquire, is carried on from motives of perfonal animofity, not from regard to public juftice); to the great fcandal and difhonour of the Commons of Great Britain in Parliament affembled, and in high contempt of their authority; to the great difturbance of the public peace and tranquillity of this kingdom; in contempt of the prefent Sovereign Lord the King, and his laws; to the evil and pernicious example of all others in the like cafe offending; and alfo againft the peace of our faid Lord the prefent King, his crown and dignity, &c. Whereupon the faid Attorney General of our faid Lord the King, who for our faid Lord the King, in this behalf, profecuteth for our faid Lord the King, prayeth the confideration of the court, here in the premifes, and that due procefs of law may be awarded againft him the faid John Stockdale, in this behalf, to make him anfwer to our faid Lord the King, touching and concerning the premifes aforefaid.

COUNSEL

COUNSEL againſt MR. STOCKDALE.

The ATTORNEY GENERAL,
The SOLICITOR GENERAL,
Mr. BEARCROFT, and Mr. WOOD.

———

SOLICITORS.

Meſſ. CHAMBERLYNE and WHITE, Solicitors for
the Affairs of his Majeſty's Treaſury.

———

COUNSEL for MR. STOCKDALE.

The Hon. THOMAS ERSKINE, and
Mr. DAYRELL.

———

SOLICITOR.

Mr. SAMUEL HARMAN, Jermyn Street.

C

[The

[The Information was opened by Mr. WOOD.]

Mr. ATTORNEY GENERAL.

MAY it pleafe your Lordfhip—Gentlemen of the Jury :

This information, which it has been my duty to file againft the defendant, John Stockdale, comes before you in confequence of an addrefs from the Houfe of Commons. This you may well fuppofe I do not mention as in any degree to influence that judgment which you are by and by to give, but I am to ftate it as a meafure which they have taken, thinking it in their wifdom, as every body muft think it—the fitteft meafure to bring before a Jury of the country, an offender of this fort againft them, and againft their honor, wifhing thereby to avoid what fometimes indeed is unavoidable, but which they wifh to avoid, whenever with propriety it can be done; the acting both as judges and accufers, that they muft neceffarily have done, had they reforted to their own powers, which are very great, and very extenfive, for the purpofe of vindicating themfelves againft infult and con-tempt, but which in the prefent inftance they wifely forbore from exercifing, thinking it better to leave this defendant to be dealt with by a fair and impartial Jury.

The

The offence which I impute to him is that of calumniating the Houfe of Commons, not in its ordinary legiflative capacity, but when acting in its accufatorial capacity, conceiving it to be their duty on adequate occafions to inveftigate the conduct of perfons in high ftations, and to leave that conduct to be judged of by the proper conftitutional tribunal, the Peers in Parliament affembled.

After due inveftigation, the Commons of Great Britain thought it their duty, as is well known, to fubmit the conduct of a fervant of this country, who governed one of its moft opulent dependencies for many years, to an enquiry before that tribunal. One fhould have thought that every good fubject of this country would have forborn imputing to the Houfe of Commons motives utterly unworthy of them, and of thofe whom they reprefent; inftead of this, to fo great a degree now has the licentioufnefs of the prefs arifen, that motives the moft unbecoming that can actuate even any individual, who may be concerned in the profecution of public juftice, are imputed to the reprefentatives of the people of this country in a body; no credit is given to them for meaning to do juftice to their country, but, on the contrary, private, perfonal, and malicious motives are imputed to the Commons of Great Britain.

When

When fuch an imputation is made upon the very firft tribunal that this country knows; namely, the great inqueft of the nation, the Commons in Parliament affembled, carrying any fubject, who they may think has offended, to the bar of the Houfe of 'Lords—I am fure you, will think this an attack fo dangerous to every tribunal, fo dangerous to the whole adminiftration of juftice, that if it be well proved, you cannot fail to give it your ftigma, by a verdict againft the defendant.

Gentlemen, The particular paffages which I fhall put my finger upon in this libel, it will now be my duty to ftate. You know very well, that it is your duty to confider of the meaning that I have imputed to thofe paffages in the information.; if you agree with me in that meaning, you convict; if you difagree with me, of courfe you acquit.

The rule of your judgment I apprehend, with fubmiffion to his Lordfhip, will be the ordinary acceptation of the words, and the plain and obvious fenfe of the feveral paffages; if there is doubt, or if there is difficulty; if there is fcrewing ingenuity, or unworthy ftraining, on the part of a public profecutor, you certainly will not pay attention to that; but, on the contrary, if he who runs may read; if the meaneft capacity muft underftand thefe words, in the plain and ob-

C 3   vious

vious fenfe, to be the fame as imputed in this information, in fuch a cafe as that, ingenuity on the other fide muft be laid afide by you, and you will not be over anxious to give a meaning to thofe words, other than the ordinary and plain one.

In my fituation, it does not become me to raife in you more indignation than the words themfelves, and the plain and fimple reading of the libel, will do : Far be it from me, if it were in my power fo to do, to provoke any undue paffions or animofity in you, againft conduct even fuch as this. The folemnity of the fituation in which I am placed on this occafion, obliges me to addrefs the intellect both of the Court and Jury, and neither their paffions nor their indignation ; for that reafon I fhall content myfelf with the few obfervations I have made, and betake myfelf merely to the words of the libel.; and leaving that with you, I am moft confident that if you follow the rule of interpretation which you always do upon fuch occafions, it cannot poffibly happen that you fhould differ from me, in the conftruction which I have put upon thefe words.

. Gentlemen, This I fhould however mention to you is a libel perhaps of a more dangerous nature than the ribaldry that we daily fee crowding every one of the prints that appear every morning upon our tables ; becaufe it is contained

contained in a work which difcovers the author of it to be by no means ignorant of the art of compofition, but certainly to be of good under-ftanding, and by no means unacquainted with letters. Therefore when calumny of this fort comes fo recommended, and addrëffing itfelf perhaps to the underftandings of the moft enlightened part of mankind—you underftand, I mean thofe who have had the beft education—it may fink deep into the minds of thofe who com-pofe the thinking and the judging part of the community ; and by mifleading them, perhaps may be of more real danger than the momentary mif-eading, or the momentary inflammation, of men's minds, by the ordinary publications of the day.

This book is intitled,

" A Review of the Principal Charges againft
" Warren Haftings, Efquire, late Governer
" General of Bengal."

One paffage in it is this :

" The Houfe of Commons has now given
" its final decifion with regard to the
" merits and demerits of Mr. Haftings.
" The grand inqueft of England have
" delivered their charges, and preferred

C 4   " their

" their impeachment; their allegations are
" referred to proof; and from the appeal
" to the collective wifdom and juftice of
" the nation in the fupreme tribunal of
" the kingdom, the queftion comes to be
" determined, whether Mr. Haftings *be*
" *guilty, or not guilty?*"

Another is this:

" What credit can we give to multiplied and
" and accumulated charges, when we find
" that they originate from mifreprefenta-
" tion and falfhood?"

Another is,

" An impeachment of *error* in *judgment,*
" with regard to the *quantum* of a fine,
" and for an intention that never was
" executed, characterizes a tribunal in-
" quifition, rather than a Court of Par-
" liament."

In another part it is faid,

" The other charges are fo infignificant in
" themfelves, or founded on fuch grofs
" mif-

" mifreprefentations, that they would not
" affect an obfcure individual, much lefs a
" public character."

And again,

" If fuccefs, in any degree, attends the de-
" figns of the accufers of Mr. Haftings,
" the voice of Britain henceforth to her
" fons, is, Go and ferve your country;
" but if you tranfgrefs the line of official
" orders, though compelled by neceffity,
" you do fo at the rifque of your fortune,
" your honour, and your life ; if you act
" with *proper prudence* againft the interefts
" of the empire, and bring calamity and
" difgrace upon your country, you have
" only to court oppofition and coalefce
" with your enemies, and you will find a
" party zealous and devoted to fupport
" you ; you may obtain a vote of thanks
" from the Houfe of Commons for your
" *fervices*, and you may *read your hiftory*
" *in the eyes of the mob*, by the light of
" bonfires and illuminations. But if, after
" èxerting,

" exerting all your efforts in the caufe of
" your country, you return, covered with
" laurels and crowned with fuccefs; if
" you preferve a loyal attachment to your
" Sovereign, you may expect the thunders
" of parliamentary vengeance; you will
" certainly be impeached, and probably be
" undone."

Another paffage is this :

The office of calm deliberate juftice, is to
" redrefs grievances as well as to punifh
" offences. It has been affirmed, that the
" natives of India have been deeply in-
" jured; but has any motion been made to
" make them compenfation for the injuries
" they have fuftained? Have the accufers
" of Mr. Haftings ever propofed to bring
" back the Rohillas to the country from
" which they were expelled? To reftore
" Cheit Sing to the Zemindary of Benares,
" or to return the Nabob of Oude the
" prefent which the Governor of Bengal
" received from him for the benefit of
" the

" the Company? Till fuch meafures are
" adopted, and in the train of negociation,
" the world has every reafon to conclude,
" that the impeachment of Mr. Haftings
" is carried on."

Now, Gentlemen, I leave you to judge what
fort of motives are imputed to the Houfe of
Commons here.

" From motives of perfonal animofity, not
" from regard to public juftice."

The general meaning, without fpecifying it in
technical language, which I have thought it my
duty to impute to thefe words, is fhortly this :
That the Houfe of Commons, without confideration, without reading, without hearing, have not
been afhamed to accufe a man of diftinguifhed
fituation; and to pervert their accufatorial character from the purpofes of deliberate, thoughtful,
confiderate juftice, to immediate hafty, paffionate,
vindictive, perfonal animofity. He reprefents,
that the better a man conducts himfelf—the more
deferving he has rendered himfelf of his country
from his paft, conduct, the more he expofes
himfelf to the vindictive proceedings of Parliament—that fuch a man will be impeached and
ruined.

In another paffage, perfonal animófity (the very words are ufed) is imputed to them as the motive of their conduct—thefe are too plain for you, Gentlemen, to differ with me in the interpretation.

I do not chufe to wafte your time, and that of my Lord, in fo plain a cafe, with much obfervation; but, hacknied as it may be, it is my duty, upon every one of thefe occafions, to remind you, Gentlemen, that the fecurity of the prefs confifts in its good regulation—if it is meant that it fhould be preferved with benefit to the public, it muft be from time to time lopped of its exceffes, by reafonable and proper verdicts of Juries, in fit and clear cafes.

EVIDENCE

EVIDENCE for the CROWN.

Mr. SOLICITOR GENERAL—We will prove that the Houſe of Commons impeached Mr. HASTINGS.

' JOSEPH WHITE, Eſq. *(ſworn.)*

Examined by Mr. SOLICITOR GENERAL.

Q. WHAT papers have you in your hand?

A. This is a copy of the Journals of the Houſe of Commons—And this is a copy of the Journals of the Houſe of Lords; *(producing them)* I examined them with the original manuſcript journals.

Mr. Erſkine. How did you examine them?

A. I examined them by one of the clerks—reading the Journal to me, and my reading the copy to him afterwards—I examined them both ways.

Mr. Erſkine. They need not be read; we all know the fact.

Mr. Solicitor General. Your Lordſhip knows we proved the publication of the paper yeſterday.

On the preceding day, upon the trial of the information againſt William Perryman, for a libel in the Morning Herald, William Gotobed was called to prove the publication of the news paper—Mr. Erſkine, for the accommodation of the witneſs, who was very ill, conſented that he ſhould at the ſame time be admitted to give his evidence relative to this trial—when his examination was as follows :

WILLIAM

I bought this pamphlet, (producing it) at Mr. Stockdales shop in Piccadilly.

Mr. Erskine. Who served you with it?

A. A boy who was in the shop.

Mr. Erskine. Whether the boy was acting regularly as a servant in the shop?

A. Mr. Stockdale was in the shop at the time I bought it, and the boy was acting as his servant.

Mr. Erskine. I admit that the witness has proved that he bought this book at the shop of Mr. Stockdale—Mr. Stockdale himself being in the shop—from a young man who acted as his servant.

The

The Hon. THOMAS ERSKINE, for the ' Defendant.

Gentlemen of the Jury,

MR. Stockdale, who is brought as a criminal before you for the publication of this book, has, by employing me as his advocate, repofed what muſt appear to many an extraordinary degree of confidence ; ſince, although he well knows that I am perſonally connected in friendſhip with moſt of thoſe, whoſe conduct and opinions are principally arraigned by its author he neverthelefs commits to my hands his defence and juſtification.

A truſt apparently ſo delicate, and ſingular, vanity is but too apt to whiſper an application of to ſome fancied merit of ones own ; but it is proper, for the honor of the Engliſh Bar, that the world ſhould know ſuch things happen to all of us daily, and of courſe; and that the defendant, without any ſort of knowledge of me, or any confidence that was perſonal, was only not afraid to follow up an accidental retainer, from the knowledge he has of the general character of the profeſſion.

Happy indeed is it for this country, that whatever intereſted diviſions may characterize other places, of which I may have occaſion to ſpeak to day, however the Councils of the higheſt depart-

ments

ments of the state may be occasionally distracted by personal considerations, they never enter these walls to disturb the administration of justice: Whatever may be *our* public principles, or the private habits of *our* lives, they never cast even a shade acrofs the path of our profeffional duties.

If this be the characteristic even of the bar of an English Court of Justice, what sacred impartiality may not every man expect from its jurors and its bench?

As, from the indulgence which the Court was yesterday pleased to give to my indispofition, this information was not proceeded on when you were attending to try it, it is probable you were not altogether inattentive to what paffed on the trial of the other indictment, profecuted also by the House of Commons; and therefore, without a re-statement of the fame principles, and a fimilar quotation of authorities to fupport them, I need only remind you of the law applicable to this fubject, as it was then admitted by the Attorney General, in conceffion to my propofitions, and confirmed by the higher authority of the Court, viz.

First, That every information or indictment must contain fuch a defcription of the crime, that the defendant may know what crime it is which he is called upon to anfwer.

Secondly,

Secondly, That the Jury may appear to be warranted in their conclusion of guilty or not guilty.

And, lastly, That the Court may see such a precise and definite transgression upon the record, as to be able to apply the punishment which judicial discretion may dictate, or which positive law may inflict.

It was admitted also to follow as a mere corollary from these propositions, that where an information charges a writing to be composed or published of and concerning the Commons of Great Britain, with an intent to bring that body into scandal and disgrace with the public, the author cannot be brought within the scope of such a charge, unless the Jury, on examination and comparison of the whole matter, written or published, shall be satisfied that the particular passages charged as criminal, when explained by the context, and considered as part of one entire work, were meant and intended by the author to vilify the House of Commons as a body, and were written of and concerning them in Parliament assembled.

These principles being settled, we are now to see what the present information is.

It charges, that the defendant, ' unlawfully, ' wickedly, and maliciously devising, contriving,

D   ' and

' and intending to afperfe, fcandalize, and vilify
' the Commons of Great Britain in Parliament
' affembled ; and moft wickedly, and audacioufly
' to reprefent their proceedings as corrupt and
' unjuft, and to make it believed and thought, as
' if the Commons of Great Britain in Parliament
' affembled, were a moft wicked, tyrannical, bafe,
' and corrupt fet of perfons, and to bring them
' into difgrace with the public.' The defendant
publifhed—*What?*—*Not* thofe latter ends of
fentences, which the Attorney General has read
from his brief, as if they had followed one another
in order in this book ;—*Not* thofe fcraps and tails
of paffages which are patched together upon this
record, and pronounced in one breath, as if they
exifted without intermediate matter in the fame
page, and without context any where.—
No—This is not the accufation, even mu-
tilated as it is : For the information charges,
that with intention to vilify the Houfe of Commons,
the defendant publifhed the whole book, defcribing
it on the record by its title :

" A Review of the Principal Charges againft
" Warren Haftings, Efq, late Governor
" General of Bengal ;"

*In which amongft other things the matter particularly
felected is to be found.* Your enquiry therefore is
not confined to, Whether the defendant publifhed
thofe

thofe felected parts of it; and whether, looking
at them as they are diftorted by the information,
they carry in fair conftruction the fenfe and
meaning which the innuendos put upon them ;
but whether the author of the *entire work,*—I fay
the author, fince, if he could defend himfelf, the
publifher unqueftionably can ; whether the author
wrote the volume which I hold in my hand, as
a free, manly, bona fide difquifition of criminal
charges againft his fellow citizen; or whether
the long eloquent difcuffion of them, which fills
fo many pages, was a mere cloak and cover for
the introduction of the fuppofed fcandal imputed
to the felected paffages; the mind of the writer all
along being intent on traducing. the Houfe of
Commons, and not on fairly anfwering thir charges
againft Mr. Haftings.

This, gentlemen, is the principal matter for
your confideration; and therefore, if after you
fhall have taken the book itfelf into the chamber,
which will be provided for you, and read the
whole of it with impartial attention ;—if after
the performance of this duty, you can return here,
and with clear confciences pronounce upon your
oaths that the impreffion made upon you by thefe
pages is that the author wrote them with the
wicked, feditious, and corrupt intentions, charged
by the information; you have then my full permiffion to find the defendant guilty. But if, on
the other hand, the general tenor of the com-

pofition

pofition fhall imprefs you with refpect for the author, and point him out to you as a man miftaken perhaps himfelf, but not feeking to deceive others :—If every line of the work fhall prefent to you an intelligent animated mind, glowing with a chriftian compaffion towards a fellow man, whom he believed to be innocent, and with a patriot zeal for the liberty of his country, which he confidered as wounded through the fides of an oppreffed fellow citizen; if this fhall be the impreffion on your confciences and underftandings, when you are called upon to deliver your verdict; then hear from me, that you not only work private injuftice, but break up the prefs of England, and furrender her rights and liberties for ever, if you convict him.

Gentlemen, to enable you to form a true judgment of the meaning of this book, and of the intention of its author, and to expofe the miferable juggle that is played off in the infor-mation, by the combination of fentences, which in the work itfelf have no bearing upon one another—I will firft give you the publication as it is charged upon the record, and prefented by the Attorney General in opening the cafe for the Crown ; and I will then, by reading the interjacent matter which is ftudioufly kept out of fight, convince you of its true interpretation. The information, beginning with the firft page of the

the book, charges, as a libel upon the Houſe of
Commons, the following ſentence:

" The Houſe of Commons has now given its
" final deciſion with regard to the merits
" and demerits of Mr. Haſtings. The
" grand inqueſt of England have de-
" livered their charges, and preferred their
" impeachment; their allegations are re-
" ferred to proof; and from the appeal
" to the collective wiſdom and juſtice of
" the nation in the ſupreme tribunal of
" the kingdom, the queſtion comes to be
" determined, whether Mr. Haſtings *be*
" *guilty or not guilty?*

It is but fair however to admit, that this firſt
ſentence, which the moſt ingenious malice
cannot torture into a criminal conſtruction, is
charged by the information rather as introductory
to what is made to follow it, than as libellous in
itſelf; for the Attorney General, from this introductory paſſage in the firſt page, goes on at
a leap to page *thirteenth*, and reads, almoſt
without a ſtop, as if it immediately followed
the other.

" What

" What credit can we give to multiplied and
" accumulated charges, when we find that
" they originate from mifreprefentation
" and falfehood ?"

From thefe two paffages thus ftanding together,
*without the intervenient matter which occupies thirteen
pages*, one would imagine that inftead of inveftigat-
ing the probability or improbability of the guilt
imputed to Mr. Haftings ; inftead of carefully examining the charges of the Commons, and the
defence of them which had been delivered before
them, or which was preparing for the Lords ;
the author immediately, and in a moment after ·
ftating the mere fact of the impeachment, had
decided that the act of the Commons originated
from mifreprefentation and falfehood.

Gentlemen, in the fame manner a veil is caft
over all that is written *in the next feven pages :*
For knowing that the conteft would help to the
true conftruction, not only of the paffages charged
before, but of thofe in the fequel of this information ; the Attorney General, aware that it would
convince every man who read it that there was
no intention in the author to calumniate the
Houfe of Commons, paffes over by another leap
to page twenty ; and in the fame manner, without
drawing his breath, and as if it directly followed
the

the two former fentences *in the 1ft and 13th pages,* reads from page 20th—

" An impeachment of error in judgment with
" regard to the quantum of a fine, and for
" an intention that never was executed,
" and never known to the offending party,
" characterifes a tribunal of inquifition
" rather·than a Court of Parliament."

From this paffage, by another vault, he'leaps over *one and thirty pages more, to page fifty one ;* where he reads the following fentence, which he mainly relies on, and upon which I fhall by and by trouble you with fome obfervations.

" Thirteen of them paffed in the Houfe of
" Commons not only without inveftigation,
" but without being read ; and the votes
" were given without enquiry, argu-
" ment, or conviction. A majority had
" determined to impeach ; oppofite parties
" met each other, and " *juftled in the*
" *dark,* to perplex the political drama, and
" and bring the hero to a tragic cata-
" ftrophe."

From

From thence, deriving new vigour from every exertion, he makes his laft grand ftride *over forty-four pages*, almoft to the end of the book, charging a fentence *in the nincty-fifth page.*

So that out of a volume of *one hundred and ten pages*, the defendant is only charged with a few fcattered fragments of fentences, picked out of *three or four.* Out of a work, confifting of about *two thoufand five hundred and thirty lines*, of manly fpirited eloquence, only *forty or fifty lines* are culled from different parts of it, and artfully put together, fo as to rear up a libel, out of a falfe context by a fuppofed connexion of fentences with one another, which are not only entirely independent, but which, when compared with their antecedents, bear a totally different conftruction.

In this manner the greateft works upon government, the moft excellent books of fcience, the facred fcriptures themfelves, might be diftorted into libels; by forfaking the general context, and hanging a meaning upon felected parts:—Thus, as in the text put by Algernon Sidney,

" The fool has faid in his heart there is no
" God;"

The Attorney General on the principle of the prefent proceeding againft this pamphlet, might indict

dict the publisher of the bible for blasphemously denying the existence of heaven, in printing

" There is no God."

For these words alone, without the context, would be selected by the information, and the bible, like this book, would be *underscored* to meet it. Nor could the defendant in such a case have any possible defence, unless the Jury were permitted to see, by the book itself, that the verse, instead of denying the existence of the Divinity, only imputed that imagination to a fool.

Gentleman, having now gone through the Attorney General's reading, the book shall presently come forward and speak for itself.

But before I can venture to lay it before you, it is proper to call your attention to how matters stood at the time of its publication; without which the author's meaning and intention cannot possibly be understood.

The Commons of Great Britain in Parliament assembled, had accused Mr. Hastiings, as Governor General of Bengal, of high crimes and misdemeanors; and their jurisdiction for that high purpose of national justice, was unquestionably competent. But it is proper you should know the nature of this
inquisitorial

inquifitorial capacity.—The Commons, in voting an impeachment, may be compared to a Grand Jury, finding a bill of indictment for the Crown: neither the one nor the other can be fuppofed to proceed, but upon the matter which is brought before them; neither of them can find guilt without accufation, nor the truth of accufation without evidence.

When therefore we fpeak of the *accufer* or *accuferers*, of a perfon indicted for any crime, although the Grand Jury are the accufers *in form*, by giving effect to the accufation; yet in common parlance we do not confider them the refponfible authors of the profecution. If I were to write of a moft wicked indictment, found againft an innocent man, which was preparing for trial, nobody who read it would conceive I meant to ftigmatize the Grand Jury that found the bill; but it would be enquired immediately, who was the profecutor, and who were the witneffes on the back of it. In the fame manner I mean to contend, that if this book is read with only common attention, the whole fcope of it will be difcovered to be this:

That in the opinion of the author, Mr. Haftings had been accufed of malicious adminiftration in India, from the heat and fpleen of political divifions in Parliament, and not from any zeal for national honour or juftice; that the impeachment

ment did not originate from Government, but from a faction banded againſt it, which, by miſre-preſentation and violence, had faſtened it on an un-willing Houſe of Commons; that, prepoſſeſſed with this ſentiment (which, howevei unfounded, makes no part of the preſent buſineſs, ſince the publiſher is not called before you for defaming individual members of the Commons, but for a contempt of the Commons as a body,) the author purſues the charges, article by article;—enters into a warm and animated vindication of Mr. Haſtings, by regular anſwers to each of them; and that, as far as the mind and ſoul of a man can be viſible, I might almoſt ſay, embodied in his writings, his inten-tion throughout the whole volume appears to have been to charge with injuſtice the private accuſers of Mr. Haſtings, and not the Houſe of Commons as a body; which undoubtedly rather reluctantly gave way to, than heartily odopted the impeachment.

This will be found to be the palpable ſcope of the book; and no man who can read Engliſh, and who at the ſame time, will have the candour and common ſenſe to take up his impreſſions from what is written in it, inſtead of bringing his own along with him to the reading of it, can poſſibly underſtand it otherwiſe.

But it may be ſaid, that admitting this to be the ſcope and deſign of the author, what right had he to canvaſs the merits of an accuſation upon
the

the records of the Commons; more efpecially while it was in the courfe of legal procedure. ,This I confefs might have been a ferious queftion; but the Commons, *as Profecutors of this Informa-tion*, feem to have waved, or forfeited their right to afk it.

Before they fent the Attorney General into this place, to punifh the publication of *anfwers* to their charges, they fhould have recollected that their own want of circumfpection in the main-tenance of their privileges, and in the protection of perfons accufed before them, had given to the public *the charges themfelves*, which fhould have been confined to their own journals.—The courfe and practice of Parliament might warrant the printing of them for the ufe of their own Mem-bers, but there the publication fhould have ftopt, and all further progrefs been refifted by authority.

If they were refolved to confider *anfwers ta their charges* as a contempt of their privileges, and to punifh the publication of them by fuch fevere profecutions, it would have well become them to have begun firft with thofe printers who by pub-lifhing *the charges themfelves* throughout the whole kingdom, or rather throughout the whole civilized world, were anticipating the paffions and judg-ments of the public againft a fubject of England upon his trial, fo as to make the publication *of*

anfwers

anfwers to them not merely a privilege, but a debt and duty to humanity and juſtice.

The Commons of Great Britain claimed and exerciſed the privileges of queſtioning the innocence of Mr. Haſtings by their impeachment ; but as, however queſtioned, it is ſtill to be preſumed and protected, until guilt is eſtabliſhed by judgment, he whom they had accuſed, had an equal claim upon their juſtice, to guard him from prejudice and miſrepreſentation until the hour of trial.

Had the Commons, therefore, by the exerciſe of their high, neceſſary and legal privileges, kept the public aloof from all canvaſs of their proceedings, by an early puniſhment of printers, who, without reſerve or ſecrecy, ſent out *the charges* into the world from a thouſand preſſes in every form of publication, they would have then ſtood upon ground to-day, from whence no argument of policy or juſtice could have removed them; becauſe nothing can be more incompatible with either, than appeals to the many upon ſubjects of judicature, which by common conſent a few are appointed to determine, and which muſt be determined by facts and principles, which the multitude have neither leiſure nor knowledge to inveſtigate. But then let it be remembered, that it is for thoſe who have the authority to accuſe and puniſh,

to

to fet the example of, and to enforce this referve, which is fo neceffary for the ends of juftice.

Courts of law therefore in England never endure the publication of *their* records ; and a profecutor of an indictment would be attached for fuch a publication; and upon the fame principle, a defendant would be punifhed for anticipating the juftice of his country, by the publication of his defence, the public being no party to it, until the tribunal appointed for its determination be open for its decifion.

Gentlemen, you have a right to take judicial notice of thefe matters, without the proof of them by witneffes ; for jurors may not only without evidence found their verdicts on facts that are notorious, but upon what they know privately themfelves, after revealing it upon oath to one another ; and therefore you are always to remember, that this book was written when the *Charges* againft Mr. Haftings, *to which it is an anfwer*, were, to the knowledge of the Commons, (for we cannot prefume our watchmen to have been afleep,) publicly hawked about in every pamphlet, magazine, and newfpaper in the kingdom.

Gentlemen, you well know with what a curious appetite thefe Charges were devoured by the
whole

whole public, interefting as they were, not only
from their importance, but from the merit of
their compofition; certainly not fo intended by
the honorable and excellent compofer to opprefs
the accufed, but becaufe the commoneft fubjects
fwell into eloquence under the touch of his fublime
genius.

Thus by the remiffnefs of the Commons, *who
are now the profecutors of this information*, a fubject
of England, who was not even charged with
contumacious refiftance to authority, much lefs
a proclaimed outlaw, and therefore fully entitled
to every protection which the cuftoms and
ftatutes of the kingdom hold out for the protection of Britifh liberty, faw himfelf pierced with
the arrows of thoufands and ten thoufands of
libels.

Gentlemen, before I venture to lay the book
before you, it muft be yet further remembered,
(for the fact is equally notorious,) that under
thefe unaufpicious circumftances, the trial of Mr.
Haftings at the bar of the Lords had actually
commenced long before its publication.

There the moft auguft and ftriking fpectacle
was daily exhibited, which the world in any age
of it ever witneffed. A vaft ftage of juftice was
erected, awful from its high authority, fplendid
from its illuftrious dignity, venerable from the
learning

learning and wifdom of its judges, captivating and affecting from the mighty concourfe of all ranks and conditions which daily flocked into it, as into a theatre of pleafure; there, when the whole public mind was at once awed and foftened to the impreffion of every human affection, there appeared, day after day, one after another, men of the moft powerful and exalted talents, eclipfing by their accufing eloquence the moft boafted harangues of antiquity; roufing the pride of national refentment, by the boldeft invectives againft broken faith, and violated treaties, and fhaking the bofom with alternate pity and horror, by the moft glowing pictures of infulted nature and humanity. Ever animated and energetic, from the love of fame, which is the inherent paffion of genius; firm and indefatigable from a ftrong prepoffeffion of the juftice of their caufe.

Gentlemen, when the author fat down to write the book now before you, all this terrible, unceafing, exhauftlefs artillery of warm zeal, matchlefs vigour of underftanding, confuming and devouring eloquence, united with the higheft dignity, was daily, and without profpect of conclufion, pouring forth upon one private unprotected man, who was bound to hear it, in the face of the whole people of England, with reverential fubmiffion and filence.

Gentlemen, I do not complain of this as I did of the publication of the Charges; becaufe it is
what

what the law allowed, and fanctioned in the
courfe of a public trial ; but when it is remembered
that we are not angels, but weak fallible men,
and that even the noble Judges of that high
tribunal are cloathed beneath their ermines
with the common infirmities of man's nature, it
will bring us all to a proper temper for confidering the book itfelf, which will in a few
moments be laid before you.

Gentlemen, it was under all thefe circumftances,
and amidft the blaze of paffion and prejudice,
which the fcene I have been endeavouring faintly
to defcribe to you might be fuppofed likely to
produce, that the author, whofe name I will now
give to you, fat down to compofe the book which
is profecuted to day as a libel.

The hiftory of it is very fhort and
natural.

The Rev. Mr. Loggan, Minifter of the Gofpel
at Leith in Scotland, a clergyman of the pureft
morals, and as you will fee by and by of very
fuperior talents, well acquainted with the human
character, and knowing the difficulty of bringing
back public opinion after it is fettled on any
fubject, took a warm, unbought, unfolicited
intereft in the fituation of Mr. Haftings, and
determined, if poffible, to arreft and fufpend the
public judgment concerning him. He felt for the

E   fituation

fituation of a fellow citizen, expofed to a trial which, whether right or wrong, is undoubtedly a fevere one; a trial, certainly not confined to a few criminal acts, like thofe we are accuftomed to, but comprehending the tranfactions of a whole life, and the complicated policys of entire nations; a trial, which had neither vifible limits to its duration, bounds to its expence, nor circum-fcribed compafs for the grafp of memory or underftanding; a trial, which had therefore broke loofe from the common forum of decifion, and had become the the univerfal topic of difcuffion in the world, fuperfeding not only every other grave purfuit, but every other fafhionable diffipation.

Gentlemen, the queftion you have there-fore to try upon all this matter, is extremely fimple; it is neither more nor lefs than this: At a time when the charges againft Mr. Haf-tings were, by the implied confent of the Com-mons, in every hand, and on every table; when by their Managers, the lightning of eloquence was inceffantly confuming him, and flafhing in the eyes of the public; when every man was with perfect impunity faying, and writing, and publifhing juft what he pleafed of the fuppofed plunderer and devaftator of nations; would it have been criminal *in Mr. Haftings himfelf* to have reminded the public that he was a native of this free land, entitled to the common protection of her juftice, and that he had a defence in his

turn

turn to offer to them, the outlines of which he. implored them in the mean time to receive, as an antidote to the unlimited and unpunifhed poifon in circulation againft him ?

Gentlemen, this is, without colour or exaggeration, the true queftion you are to decide. For I affert, without the hazard of contradiction, that if Mr. Haftings himfelf could have ftood juftified or excufed in your eyes, for publifhing this volume in his own defence, the author, if he wrote it *bona fide* to defend him, muft ftand equally excufed and juftified; and if the author be juftified, the publifher cannot be criminal, unlefs you had evidence that it was publifhed by him, with a different fpirit and intention from thofe in which it was written. The queftion therefore is correctly what I juft now ftated it to be : Could *Mr. Haftings* have been condemned to infamy for writing this book ?

Gentlemen, I tremble with indignation, to be driven to put fuch a queftion in England. Shall it be endured, that a fubject of this country, inftead of being arraigned and tried for fome fingle act in her ordinary courts, where the accufation, as foon at leaft as it is made public, is followed within a few hours by the decifion, may be impeached by the Commons for the tranfactions of twenty years, that the accufation fhall fpread as wide as the region of letters, and the accufed

fhall

ſhall ſtand day after day, and year after year, as a ſpectacle before the public, which ſhall be kept in a perpetual ſtate of inflammation againſt him; yet that he ſhall not, without the ſevereſt penalties, be permitted to ſubmit any thing to the judgment of mankind in his defence. If this be law (which it is for you to day to decide), ſuch a man has no trial; that great hall, built by our fathers for Engliſh juſtice, is no longer a court, but an altar; and an Engliſhman, inſtead of being judged in it by GOD AND HIS COUNTRY, is A VICTIM AND A SACRIFICE,—Gentlemen, you will carefully remember, that I am not preſuming to queſtion either the right or the duty of the Commons of Great Britain to impeach; neither am I arraigning the propriety of their ſelecting, as they have done, the moſt extraordinary perſons for ability which the age has produced to manage their impeachment. Much leſs am I cenſuring the Managers themſelves, charged with the conduct of it before the Lords, who were undoubtedly bound by their duty to the houſe, and to the public, to expatiate upon the crimes of the perſons whom they had accuſed.

None of theſe points are queſtioned by me, nor are in this place queſtionable. I only deſire to have it decided, whether if the Commons, when national expediency happens to call in their judgment for an impeachment, ſhall, inſtead of keeping it on their own records, and carrying it with due
ſolemnity

folemnity to the peers for trial, permit it without cenfure and punifhment to be fold like a common news paper in the fhop of my client, fo crowded with their own members, that no plain man, without privilege of Parliament, can hope even for a fight of the fire in a winter's day; every man buying it, reading it, and commenting upon it ; the gentleman himfelf who is the object of it, or his friend in his abfence, may not, without ftepping beyond the bounds of Englifh freedom; put a copy of what is thus publifhed into his pocket, and fend back to the very fame fhop for publication a bona fide, rational, able anfwer to it, in order that the bane and antidote may circulate together, and the public be kept ftraight till the day of decifion.

Gentlemen, if you think that this common duty of felf-prefervation, in the accufed himfelf, which nature writes as a law upon the hearts of even favages and brutes, is neverthelefs too high a privilege to be enjoyed by an impeached and fuffering Englifhman ; or if you think it beyond the office of humanity and juftice, when brought home to the hand of a brother or a friend, you will fay fo by your verdict of GUILTY—The decifion will then be *yours ;* and the confolation-*mine,* that I laboured to avert it. A very fmall part of the mifery which will follow from it, is likely to light upon *me ;* the reft will be divided

E 3   amongft

amongſt *yourſelves and your children.* Gentlemen, I obſerve plainly, and with infinite ſatisfaction, that you are ſhocked and offended at my even ſuppoſing it poſſible you ſhould pronounce ſuch a deteſtable judgment ; and that you only require of me to make out to your ſatisfaction *(as I promiſed)* that the real ſcope and object of this book is a bona fide defence of Mr. Haſtings, and *not a cloak and cover for ſcandal on the Houſe of Commons.* Gentlemen, I engage to do this, and I engage for nothing more ; I ſhall make an open manly defence. I mean to torture no expreſſions from their natural conſtructions, to diſpute no innuendos on the record, ſhould any of them have a fair application ; nor to conceal from your notice any unguarded intemperate expreſſions, which may perhaps be found to chequer the vigorous and animated career of the work. Such a conduct might by accident, ſhelter the defendant ; but it would be the ſurrender of the very principle on which alone the liberty of the Engliſh preſs can ſtand ; and I ſhall never defend any man from a temporary impriſonment, by the permanent loſs of my own liberty, and the ruin of my country. I mean therefore to ſubmit to you, that though you ſhould find a few lines in page thirteen, or twenty-one ; a few more in page fifty-one, and ſome others in other places ; containing expreſſions bearing on the Houſe of Commons, even as a body, which, if written as independent paragraphs by themſelves, would

would be indefensible libels ; yet that you have a right to pass them over in judgment, provided the substance clearly appears to be a bona fide conclusion, arising from the honest investigation of a subject which it was lawful to investigate, and the questionable expressions, the visible effusion of a zealous temper, engaged in an honourable and legal pursuit. After this preparation I am not afraid to lay the book in its genuine state before you.

The Pamphlet begins thus,

" THE House of Commons has now given
" its final decision with regard to the
" merits and demerits of Mr. Hastings.
" The grand inquest of England have deli-
" vered their charges, and preferred their
" impeachment ; their allegations are re-
" ferred to proof ; and from the appeal to
" the collective wisdom and justice of the
" nation in the supreme tribunal of the
" kingdom, the question comes to be de-
" termined, whether Mr. Hastings *be guilty*
" *or not guilty ?*"

Now if immediately after what I have just read to you, (which is the first part charged by the information) the author had said

E 4

" Will

" Will accufations, built on fuch a bafelefs
" fabric, prepoffefs the public in favour
" of the impeachment? What credit can
" we give to multiplied and accumulated
" charges, when we find that they originate
" from mifreprefentation and falfehood?

Every man would have been juftified in pronouncing that he was attacking the Houfe of Commons,
becaufe the groundlefs accufations mentioned in
the fecond fentence, could have no reference but
to the Houfe itfelf, mentioned by name in the firft
and only fentence which preceded it.

But, Gentlemen, to your aftonifhment, I will
now read what intervenes between thefe two paffages; from which you will fee, beyond a poffibility
of doubt, that the author never meant to calumniate the Houfe of Commons, but to fay that the
accufation of Mr. Haftings before the whole Houfe
grew out of a Committe of Secrefy eftablifhed fome
years before, and was afterwards brought forward
by the fpleen of private enemies, and a faction in
the Government. This will appear, not only from
the grammatical conftruction of the words, but
from what is better than words; from the meaning which a perfon writing as the friend of
Mr. Haftings muft be fuppofed to have intended to
convey. Why fhould fuch a friend attack the
Houfe

Houfe of Commons? Will any man gravely tell me, that the Houfe of Commons, as a body, ever wifhed to impeach Mr. Haftings? Do we not all know that they conftantly hung back from it, and hardly knew where they were, or what to do, when they found themfelves entangled with it? My learned friend the Attorney General is a member of this affembly; perhaps he may tell you by and by what he thought of it, and whether he ever marked any difpofition in the majority of the Commons hoftile to Mr. Haftings. But why fhould I diftrefs my friend by the queftion; the fact is fufficiently notorious; and what I am going to read from the book itfelf, (which is left out in the information,) is too plain for controverfy.

" Whatever may be the event of the im-
" peachment, the proper exercife of fuch
" power is a valuable privilege of the
" Britifh conftitution, a formidable guar-
" dian of the public liberty, and the dig-
" nity of the nation. *The only danger is,*
" *that from the influence of faction, and the*
" *awe which is annexed to great names,*
" *they may be prompted to determine before*
" *they inquire, and to pronounce judgment*
" *without examination,*"

Here

Here is the clue to the whole pamphlet. The author trufts to and refpects the Houfe of Commons, but is afraid their mature and juft examination will be difturbed by *faction*.

Now, does he mean Government, by *faction?* Does he mean the majority of the Commons, by *faction?* Will the Houfe, which is the profecutor here, fanction that application of the phrafe; or will the Attorney General admit the majority to be the true innuendo of *faction?* I wifh he would ; I fhould then have gained fomething at leaft by this extraordinary debate; but I have no expectation of the fort ; fuch a conceffion would be too great a facrifice to any profecution, at a time when every thing is confidered as faction that difturbs the repofe of the Minifter in Parliament. But indeed, Gentlemen, fome things are too plain for argument. The author certainly means *my friends,* who, whatever qualifications may belong to them, muft be contented with the appellation of *faction,* while they oppofe the Minifter in the Houfe of Commons ; but the Houfe, having given this meaning to the phrafe of faction for its own purpofes, cannot in decency change the interpretation, in order to convict my client. I take that to be beyond the privilege of Parliament.

The fame bearing upon individual members of the Commons, *and not on the Commons as a body,* is obvious throughout. Thus, after faying, in
page

page 9, that the Eaſt-India Company had thanked Mr. Haſtings for his meritorious ſervices (which is unqueſtionably true,) he adds,

" That mankind would abide by their deli-
" berate deciſion, rather than by the in-
" temperate aſſertion of a Committee."

This he writes after the impeachment was found by the Commons at large; but he takes no account of their proceedings; imputing the whole to the original Committee, *i. e. the Committee of Secrecy;* ſo called, I ſuppoſe, from their being the authors of twenty volumes in folio, which will remain a ſecret to all, poſterity, as nobody will ever read them. The ſame conſtruction is equally plain from what immediately follows:

" The report of the Committee of Secrecy
" alſo ſtates, that the happineſs of the na-
" tive inhabitants of India has been deeply
" affected, their confidence in Engliſh faith
" and lenity ſhaken and impaired, and the
" character of this nation wantonly and
" wickedly degraded."

Here again you are groſsly miſled by the omiſſion of near *twenty-one pages.* For the author, though he is here ſpeaking of this Committe *by name,*

name, which brought forward the charges to the notice of the Houfe, and which he continues to do onward to the next felected paragraph ; yet, by arbitrarily finking the whole context, he is taken to be fpeaking of the Houfe as a *body*, when, in the paffage next charged by the information, he reproaches the *accufers* of Mr. Haftings. Although, fo far is he from confidering them as the charges of the Houfe of Commons, that in the very fame page he fpeaks of them as the charges, not even of the Committee, but of Mr. Burke alone, the moft active and intelligent member of that body ; and as having been circulated in India by a relation of that gentleman :

" The charges of Mr. Burke have been car-
" ried to Calcutta, and carefully circulated
" in India*."

* " Mr. William Burke, a coufin of the Member of
" Parliament, undertook this *friendly* office.

Now, if we were confidering thefe paffages of the work as calumniating a body of gentlemen, many of whom I muft be fuppofed highly to refpect, or as reflecting upon my worthy friend whofe name I have mentioned, it would give rife to a totally different enquiry, which it is neither my duty nor your's to agitate ; but furely, the more that confideration obtrudes itfelf upon us, the more clearly it demonftrates, that the author's whole direction was againft the individual ac-

cufers

cufers of Mr. Haftings, and not againft the Houfe of Commons, which merely trufted to the matter they had collected.

Although, from a caution which my fituation dictates as reprefenting another, I have thought it my duty thus to point out to you the real intention of the author, as it appears by the fair conftruction of the work, yet I proteft, that in my own apprehenfion it is very immaterial, whether he fpeaks of the Committee or of the Houfe, provided you fhall think the whole volume a bona fide defence of Mr. Haftings. This is the great point I am, by all my obfervations, endeavouring to eftablifh, and which I think no man who reads the following fhort paffages can doubt. Very intelligent perfons have indeed confidered them, if founded in facts, to render every other amplification unneceffary. The firft of them is as follows :

" It was known, at that time, that Mr.
" Haftings had not only defcended from
" a public to a private ftation, but that he
" was perfecuted with accufations and im-
" peachments. But none of thefe *fuffering*
" *millions* have fent their complaints to this
" country : not a figh nor a groan has been
" wafted from India to Britain. On the
" contrary, teftimonies the moft honour-
" able

" able to the character and merit of Mr,
" Haftings, have been tranfmitted by
" thofe very princes whom he has been
" fuppofed to have loaded with the deepeft
" injuries."

Here, Gentlemen, we muft be permitted to
paufe together a little ; for in examining whether
thefe pages were written as an honeft anfwer to the
charges of the Commons, or as a proftituted defence of a notorious criminal, whom the writer
believed to be guilty, *truth becomes material at
every ftep.* For if *in any inftance* he be detected
of a *wilful* mifreprefentation, he is no longer an
object of your attention.

Will the Attorney General proceed then to
detect the hypocrify of our author, by giving us
fome detail of the proofs by which thefe perfonal
enormities have been eftablifhed, and which the
writer muft be fuppofed to have been acquainted
with ? I afk this as the defender of *Mr. Stockdale,*
not of Mr. Haftings, with whom I have no concern. I am forry, indeed, to be fo often obliged
to repeat this proteft ; but I really feel myfelf em-
barraffed with thofe repeated coincidencies of defence which thicken on me as I advance, and
which were, no doubt, overlooked by the Commons when they directed this interlocutory enquiry into his conduct.

I afk

I afk then, *as counfel for* . Mr. *Stockdale,* Whether, when a great ftate criminal is brought for juftice at an immenfe expence 'to the public, accufed of the moft oppreffive cruelties, 'and charged with the robbery of princes and the de-. ftruction of nations ; it is not open to any one to afk, Who are his accufers ? What are the fources and the authorities of thefe fhocking complaints?— Where are the ambaffadors or memorials of thofe princes whofe revenues he has plundered?—Where. are the witneffes for thofe unhappy men in whofe perfons the rights of humanity have been violated ? —How deeply buried is the blood of the innocent that it does not rife up in retributive judgment to confound the guilty! Thefe furely are queftions, which, when a fellow-citizen is upon a long, pain- ful, and expenfive trial, humanity has a right to propofe ; which the plain fenfe of the moft unlet- tered man may be expected to dictate, and which all hiftory muft provoke from the more en- lightened.

When CICERO impeached VERRES before the great tribunal of Rome of fimilar cruelties and depredations in *her* provinces, the Roman people were not left to fuch enquiries. ALL SICILY furrounded the forum, demanding juftice upon her plunderer and fpoiler, with tears and imprecations. It was not by the eloquence of the *orator*, but by the cries and tears of the miferable, that Cicero prevailed in that illuftrious caufe.

. VERRES

VERRES fled from the oaths of his accufers and their witneffes, and not from the voice of TULLY ; who, to prefcrve the fame of his eloquence, publifhed the five celebrated fpeeches which were never delivered againft the criminal, becaufe he had fled from the city, appalled with the fight of the perfecuted and the oppreffed.

It may be faid, that the cafes of Sicily and India are widely different; perhaps they may; whether they are or not is foreign to my purpofe. I am not bound to deny the poffibility of anfwers to fuch queftions; I am only vindicating *the right to afk them*. Gentlemen, the author in the other paffage which I marked out to your attention goes on thus :

" Sir John Macpherfon, and Lord Corn-
" wallis, his fucceffors in office, has given
" the fame voluntary tribute of approba-
" tion to his meafures as Governor Ge-
" neral of India. A letter from the former,
" dated the 10th of Auguft, 1786, gives
" the following account of our dominions
" in Afia : ' The native inhabitants of this
" kingdom are the happieft and beft pro-
" tected fubjects in India ; our native
" allies and tributaries confide in our protection;

" tection ; the country powers are afpiring
" to the friendfhip of the Englifh ; and
" from the King of Tidore, towards New
" Guinea, to Timur Shaw, on the banks
" of the Indus, there is not a ftate that has
" not *lately* given us proofs of confidence
" and refpect."

Still purfuing the fame teft of fincerity, let us
examine this defenfive allegation.

Will the Attorney General fay that he does
not believe fuch a letter from Lord Cornwallis
ever exifted ? No : For he knows that it is as
authentic as any document from India upon the
table of the Houfe of Commons. What then is
the letter ? The native inhabitants of this kingdom, fays Lord Cornwallis, (writing from the very
fpot,) are the happieft and beft protected fubjects
in India, &c. &c. &c. The inhabitants of *this
kingdom! Of what kingdom ?* Why of the very
kingdom which Mr. Haftings had juft returned
from governing for thirteen years, and for the
mif-government and defolation of which, he ftands
every day as a criminal, or rather as a fpectacle,
before us. This is matter for ferious reflection ;
and fully entitles the author to put the queftion
which immediately follows :

F   " Does

" Does this authentic account of the admi-
" niftration of Mr. Haftings, and of the
" ftate of India, correfpond with the
" gloomy picture of defpotifm and defpair,
" drawn by the Committee of Secrecy?"

Had that picture been even drawn by the Commons itfelf, he would have been fully juftified in
afking this queftion ; but you obferve it has no
bearing on it ; the laft words not only entirely
deftroy that interpretation, but alfo the meaning
of the very next paffage, which is felected by the
information as criminal, viz.

" What credit can we give to multiplied and
" accumulated charges, when we find that
" they originate from mifreprefentation
" and falfehood?"

This paffage, which is charged as a libel on the
Commons, when thus compared with its immediate antecedent, can bear but one conftruction.
It is impoffible to contend that it charges mifreprefentation on the Houfe of Commons that
found the impeachment, but upon the Committee
of Secrecy juft before adverted to, who were fuppofed to have felected the matter, and brought it
before the whole Houfe for judgment.

I do

I do not mean, as I have often told you, to vindicate any calumny on that honorable Committee, or upon any individual of it, any more than upon the Commons at large; but the defendant is not charged by this information with any fuch offences.

Let me here paufe once more to afk you, Whether the book in its genuine ftate, as far as we have advanced in it, makes the fame impreffion on your minds now, as when it was firft read to you in detached paffages ; and whether, if I were to tear off the firft part of it which I hold in my hand, and give it to you as an entire work, the firft and laft paffages which have been felected as libels on the Commons, would now appear to be fo when blended with the interjacent parts. I do not afk your anfwer. I fhall have it in your verdict. The queftion is only put to direct your attention in purfuing the remainder of the volume to this main point,—Is it an honeft ferious defence? For this purpofe, and as an example for all others, I will read the author's entire anfwer to the firft article of charge concerning Cheit Sing, the Zemindar of Benares, and leave it to your impartial judgments to determine, whether it be a mere cloak and cover for the flander imputed by the information to the concluding fentence of it, which is the only part attacked ; or whether, on the contrary, that con-

F 2   clufion

clufion itfelf, when embodied with what goes before
·it, does not ftand explained and juftified ?

" The firft article of impeachment, (continues
" our author), is concerning Cheit Sing, the
" Zemindar of Benares. Bulwant Sing,
" the father of this Rajah, was merely an
" *Aumil,* or farmer and colle&tor of the
" revenues for Sujah ul Dowlah, Nabob
" of Oude, and Vizir of the Mogul em-
" pire. When, on the deceafe of his.
" father, Cheit Sing was confirmed in the
" office of colle&tor for the Vizir, he paid
" 200,000 pounds as a gift or nuzzeranah,
" and an additional rent of 30,000 pounds.
" per annum.

" As the father was no more than an *Aumil,*
" the fon fucceeded only to his rights and
" pretenfions. But by a funnud granted
" to him by the Nabob Sujah Dowlah in
" September 1773, through the influence of
· " Mr. Haftings, he acquired a legal title to
" property in the land, and was raifed
" from the office of *Aumil* to the rank of
" Zemindar.

" Zemindar, About four years after the
" death of Bulwant Sing, the Governor
" General and Council of Bengal obtained
" the fovereignty paramount of the pro-
" vince of Benares. On the transfer of
" this fovereignty the Governor and Coun-
" cil propofed a new grant to Cheit Sing,
" confirming his former privileges, and
" conferring upon him the addition of the
" fovereign rights of the mint, and the
" powers of criminal juftice with regard to
" life and death. He was then recognized
" by the Company as one of their Zemin-
" dars; a tributary fubject, or feudatory
" vaffal, of the Britifh empire in Indoftan.
" The feudal fyftem, which was formerly
" fuppofed to be peculiar to our Gothic
" anceftors, has always prevailed in the
" Eaft. In every defcription of that form
" of government, notwithftanding acci-
" dental variations, there are two affoci-
" ations expreffed or underftood; one for
" internal fecurity, the other for external
" defence. The King or Nabob, confers

" protection

" protection on the feudatory baron as tri-
" butary prince, on condition of an annual
" revenue in the time of peace, and of
" military fervice, partly commutable for
" money, in the time of war. The feudal
" incidents in the middle ages in Europe,
" the fine paid to the fuperior on *marriage*,
" *wardſhip*, *relief*, &c. correfpond to the
" annual tribute in Afia. Military fervice
" in war, and extraordinory aids in the
" event of extraordinary emergencies, were
" common to both *.

" When

" * Notwithſtanding this analogy, the powers and pri-
" vileges of a Zemindar have never been fo well
" afcertained and defined as thofe of a Baron in the
" feudal ages. Though the office has ufually defcended
" to the pofterity of the Zemindar, under the ceremony
" of fine and inveſtiture, a material decreafe in the
" cultivation, or decline in the population of the
" diſtrict, has fometimes been confidered as a ground
" to difpoffefs him. When Zemindars have failed in
" their engagements to the ſtate, though not to the
" extent to juſtify expulfion, fupervifors have been
" often fent into the Zemindaries, who have farmed
" out the lands, and exercifed authority under the
" Duannee laws, independent of the Zemindar.
" Thefe circumſtances ſtrongly mark their *dependence*
" on the Nabob. About a year after the departure

" of

" When the Governor General of Bengal in
" 1778, made an extraordinary demand on
" the Zemindar of Benares for five lacks of
" rupees, the Britifh empire, in that part of
" the world, was furrounded with enemies,
" which threatened its deftruction. In 1779,
" a general confederacy was formed among
" the great powers of Indoftan for the ex-
" pulfion of the Englifh from their Afiatic
" dominions. At this crifis the expectation
" of a French armament augmented the
" general calamities of the country. Mr.
" Haftings is charged by the Committee,
" with making his firft demand under the

" of Mr. Haftings from India, the queftion concerning
" the rights of Zemindars was agitated at great length
" in Calcutta, and after the fulleft and moft accurate
" inveftigation, the Governor General and Council
" gave it as their deliberate opinion to the Court of
" Directors, that the property of the foil is not in the
" Zemindar, but in the government; and that a Ze-
" mindar is merely an officer of government appointed
" to collect its revenues. Cheit Sing underftood him-
" felf to ftand in this predicament. ' I am,' faid he,
" on various occafions, ' the fervant of the Circar
" (government), and ready to obey your orders.' The
" name and office of Zemindar is not of Hindoo, but
" Mogul inftitution."

F 4   " falfe

" falfe pretence that hoftilities had com-
" menced with France. Such an infidious
" attempt, to pervert a meritorious action
" into a crime, is new even in the hiftory
" of impeachments. On the 7th of July
" 1778, Mr. Haftings received private
" intelligence from an Englifh merchant at
" Cairo, that war had been declared by
" Great Britain on the 23d of March, and
" by France on the 30th of April. Upon
" this intelligence, confidered as authentic,
" it was determined to attack all the French
" fettlements in India. The information was
" afterwards found to be premature; but in
" the latter end of Auguft, a fecret difpatch
" was received from England, authorifing
" and appointing Mr. Haftings to take the
" meafures which he had already adopted in
" the preceding month. The Directors and
" the board of Controul have expreffed
" their approbation of this tranfaction, by
" liberally rewarding Mr. Baldwyn, the
" merchant, for fending the earlieft intel-
" ligence he could procure to Bengal. It
" was

" was *two days* after Mr. Haftings's infor-
" mation of the French war, that he
" formed the refolution of exacting the
" five lacks of rupees from Cheit Sing, and
" would have made *fimilar exactions* from
" all the dependencies of the Company in
" India, had they been in the fame circum-
" ftances. The fact is, that the great Ze-
" mindars of Bengal pay as much to
" Government as their lands can afford:
" Cheit Sing's collections were above fifty
" lacks, and his rent not twenty-four.

" The right of calling for extraordinary aids
" and military fervice in times of danger
" being univerfally eftablifhed in India, as
" it was formerly in Europe during the
" feudal times, the fubfequent conduct of
" Mr. Haftings is explained and vindicated.
" The Governor General and Council of
" Bengal having made a demand upon a
" tributary Zemindar for three fucceffive
" years, and that demand having been re-
" fifted by their vaffal, they are juftified in
" his punifhment. The neceffities of the
" Company,

" Company, in consequence of the critical
" situation of their affairs in 1781, calling
" for a high fine; the ability of the Ze-
" mindar, who poffeffed near two crores of
" rupees in money and jewels, to pay the
" fum required; his backwardnefs to com-
" ply with the demands of his fuperiors ;
" his difaffection to the Englifh intereft,
" and defire of revolt, which even then
" began to appear, and were afterwards
" confpicuous, fully juftify Mr. Haftings
" in every fubfequent ftep of his conduct.
" In the whole of his proceedings it is mani-
" feft that he had not early formed a defign
" hoftile to the Zemindar, but was regu-
" lated by events which he could neither
" forefee nor controul. When the necef-
" fary meafures which he had taken for
" fupporting the authority of the Com-
" pany, by punifhing a refractory vaffal,
" were thwarted and defeated by the bar-
" barous maffacre of the Britifh troops, and
" the rebellion of Cheit Sing, the appeal
" was made to arms, an unavoidable revo-
" lution

" lution took place in Benares, and the
" Zemindar became the author of his own
" deftruction.

Here follows the concluding paffage, which is
arraigned by the information.

" The decifion of the Houfe of Commons on
" this charge againft Mr. Haftings, is one
" of the moft fingular to be met with in the
" annals of Parliament. The Minifter,
" who was followed by the majority, vin-
" dicated him in every thing that he had
" *done,* and found him blameable only for
" what he *intended* to *do;* juftified every
" ftep of his *conduct,* and criminated his
" propofed *intention* of converting the
" crimes of the Zemindar to the benefit of
" the ftate, by a fine of fifty lacks of ru-
" pees. An impeachment of *error* in
" *judgment* with regard to the *quantum* of
" a fine, and for an *intention* that never was
" *executed,* and never known to the offend-
" ing party, characterifes a tribunal *inqui-*
" *fition* rather than a Court of Parliament."

Gentlemen,

Gentlemen, I am ready to admit that this sentiment might have been expressed in language more reserved and guarded; but you will look to the sentiment itself, rather than to its dress; to the mind of the writer, and not to the bluntness with which he may happen to express it. It is obviously the language of a warm man, engaged in the honest defence of his friend, and who is brought to what he thinks a just conclusion in argument, which perhaps becomes offensive in proportion to its truth. Truth is undoubtedly no warrant for writing what is reproachful of any *private* man; for if a member of society lives within the law, then if he offends it is against God alone, and man has nothing to do with him; and if he transgress the laws, the libeller should arraign him before them, instead of presuming to try him himself. But as to writings on *general subjects*, which are not charged as an infringement on the rights of indi-viduals, but as of a seditious tendency, it is far otherwise.

When, in the progress either of legislation or of high national justice in Parliament, they who are amenable to no law, are supposed to have adopted through mistake or error a principle which, if drawn into precedent, might be dangerous to the public; I shall not admit it to be a libel *in the course of a legal and bona fide publication,* to state that such a principle had *in fact* been adopted; for the people of England are not to be kept in the dark, touching

touching the proceedings of their own reprefentatives. Let us therefore coolly examine this fuppofed offence, and fee what it amounts to.——

Firft, Was not the conduct of the Right Honorable Gentleman, whofe name is here mentioned, exactly what it is reprefented? Will the Attorney General, who was prefent in the Houfe of Commons, fay that it was not? Did not the minifter vindicate Mr. Haftings in what he *had done*, and was not his confent to that article of the impeachment founded on the intention of levying a fine on the Zemindar for the fervice of the ftate, beyond the quantum which he the minifter thought reafonable?

What elfe is this but an impeachment of error in judgment, in the quantum of a fine.

So much for the firft part of the fentence, which, regarding Mr. Pitt only, is foreign to our purpofe; and as to the laft part of it, which imputes the fentiments of the minifter to the majority that followed him with their votes on the queftion, that appears to me to be giving handfome credit to the majority for having voted from conviction and not from curtefy to the minifter. To have fuppofed otherwife, I dare not fay, would have been a more *natural* libel, but it would certainly have been a greater one—The fum and fubftance therefore of the paragraph is only this: that an impeach-
                                                        ment

ment for an error in judgment, is not confiftent with the theory or the practice of the English Government.—So say I.

I fay without referve, fpeaking merely in the abftract, and not meaning to decide upon the merits of Mr. Haftings' caufe, that an impeachment for an error in judgment is contrary to the whole fpirit of Englifh criminal juftice, which, though not binding on the Houfe of Commons, ought to be a guide to their proceedings. I fay.that their extraordinary jurifdiction of impeachment, ought never to be affumed to expofe error, or to fcourge misfortune, but to hold up a terible example to corruption and *wilful* abufe of authority by extra legal pains.

If public men are always punifhed with due feverity, when the fource of their mifconduct appears to have been *felfifhly, corrupt, and criminal,* the public can never fuffer when their errors are treated with gentlenefs ; for no man from fuch protection to the magiftrate can think lightly of the charge of magiftracy itfelf, when he fees, by the language of the faving judgment, that the only title to it is an honeft and zealous intention.

Gentlemen, if at this moment, or indeed in any other in the whole courfe of our hiftory, the people of England were to call upon every man in this impeaching Houfe of Commons, who had given

his

his voice on public queſtions, or acted in authority civil or military, to anſwer for the iſſues of our councils and our wars, and if honeſt ſingle intentions for the public ſervice were refuſed as anſwers to impeachments, we ſhould have many relations to mourn for, and many friends to deplore. For my own part, Gentlemen, I feel I hope for my country as much as any man that inhabits it : but I would rather ſee it fall, and be buried in its ruins, than lend my voice to wound any miniſter, or other reſponſible perſon, however unfortunate, who had fairly followed the lights of his underſtanding and the dictates of his conſcience for their preſervation.

Gentlemen, this is no theory of mine, it is the language of Engliſh law, and the protection which it affords to every man in office, from the higheſt to the loweſt truſts of Government.

In no one inſtance that can be named, foreign or domeſtic, did the Court of King's Bench ever interpoſe its extraordinary juriſdiction, by information againſt any magiſtrate for the wideſt departure from the rule of his duty, without *the plaineſt and cleareſt proof of corruption.* To every ſuch application, not ſo ſupported, the conſtant anſwer has been, Go to a Grand Jury with your complaint. God forbid that a magiſtrate ſhould ſuffer from an error in judgment, if his purpoſe was honeſtly to diſcharge his truſt. We cannot ſtop the ordinary courſe of juſtice; but wherever the

Court

Court has a difcretion, fuch a magiftrate is entitled to its protection. I appeal to the noble Judge, and to every man who hears me, for the truth and univerfality of this pofition. And it would be a ftrange folecifm indeed to affert, that in a cafe where the fupreme court of criminal juftice in the nation would refufe to interpofe an *extraordinary* though a legal jurifdiction, on the principle that the ordinary execution of the laws fhould never be exceeded, but for the punifhment of malignant guilt, the Commons in their judicial capacity, growing out of the fame conftitution, fhould reject that principle, and ftretch them ftill further by a jurifdiction ftill more *eccentric.*—Many impeachments have taken place, becaufe the law *could not* adequately punifh the objects of them; but whoever heard of one being fet on foot becaufe the law upon principle *would not* punifh them?—Many impeachments have been adopted for a higher example than a profecution in the ordinary Courts, but furely never for a different example.—The matter therefore, in the offenfive paragraph, is not only an indifputable truth, but a truth in the propagation of which we are all deeply concerned.

Whether Mr. Haftings, in the inftance, acted from corruption, or from zeal for his employers, is what I have nothing to do with; it is to be decided in judgment; my duty ftops with wifhing him, as I do, an honourable deliverance.—Whether the Minifter or the Commons meant to found this article

article of the impeachment, on mere error without corruption, is likewife foreign to the purpofe. The author could only judge from what was faid and done on the occafion. He only fought to guard the principle which is a common intereft, and the rights of Mr. Haftings under it; and was therefore juftified in publifhing, that an impeachment, founded in error in judgment, was to all intents and purpofes illegal, unconftitutional, and unjuft.—Gentlemen, it is now time for us to return again to the work under examination.

The author, having difcuffed the whole of the firft article through fo many pages, without even the imputation of an incorrect or intemperate ex-preffion, except in the concluding paffage, the meaning of which I truft I have explained, goes on with the fame earneft difpofition to the dif-cuffion of the fecond charge refpecting the prin-ceffes of Oude, which occupies eighteen pages, not one fyllable of which the Attorney General has read, and on which there is not even a glance at the Houfe of Commons; the whole of this anfwer is indeed fo far from being a mere cloak for the introduction of flander, that I aver it to be one of the moft mafterly pieces of writing I ever read in my life: from thence he goes on to the charge of contracts and falaries, which occupies five pages more, in which *there is not a glance at the Houfe of Commons, nor a word read by the Attorney General*—He afterwards defends Mr. Haftings

G   againft

againſt the charges reſpecting the opium contracts. *Not a glance at the Houſe of Commons ; not a word by the Attorney General.* And in ſhort, in this manner he goes on with the others to the end of the book.

Now is it poſſible for any human being to believe, that a man, having no other intention than to vilify the Houſe of Commons *(as this information charges),* ſhould yet keep his mind thus fixed and ſettled as the needle to the pole, upon the ſerious merits of Mr. Haſtings defence, without ever ſtraying into matter even queſtionable, except in the two or three ſelected parts out of two or three hundred pages. This is a forbearance which could not have exiſted, if calumny and detraction had been the malignant objects which led him to the enquiry and publication. The whole fallacy therefore ariſes from holding up to view a few detached paſſages, and carefully concealing the general tenor of the book.

Having now finiſhed moſt, if not all of theſe *critical* obſervations, which it has been my duty to make upon this unfair mode of proſecution; it is but a tribute of common juſtice to the Attorney General, (and which my perſonal regard for him makes it more pleaſant to ſay,) that none of my commentaries reflect in the moſt diſtant manner upon him ; nor upon the Solicitor for the

the Crown, who fits near me, who is a perfon of the moft correct honour;—far from it. The Attorney General having orders to profecute, in confequence of the addrefs of the Houfe to his Majefty, had no choice in the mode; no means at all of keeping the profecutors before you in countenance, but by the courfe which has been purfued; but fo far has he been from enlifting into the caufe thofe prejudices, which it is not difficult to flide into a bufinefs originating from fuch exalted authority, he has honorably guarded you againft them; preffing indeed feverely upon my client, with the weight of his ability, but not with the glare and trappings of his high office.

Gentlemen, I wifh that my ftrength would enable me to convince you of the author's finglenefs of intention, and of the merit and ability of his work, by reading the whole that remains of it. But my voice is already nearly exhaufted; I am forry my client fhould be a fufferer by my infirmity; one paffage however is too ftriking and important to be paffed over; the reft I muft truft to your private examination. The author having difcuffed all the charges, article by article, fums them all up with this ftriking appeal to his readers.

" The authentic ftatement of facts which has
" been given, and the arguments which have
" been employed, are, I think, fufficient to

" vindicate

" vindicate the character and conduct of
" Mr. Haftings, even on the maxims of
" European policy. When he was ap-
" pointed Governor General of Bengal, he
" was invefted with a difcretionary power
" to promote the interefts of the India
" Company, and of the Britifh empire in
" that quarter of the globe. The general
" inftructions fent to him from his con-
" ftituents were, ' That in all your deli-
" berations and refolutions, you make the
" fafety and profperity of Bengal your
" principal object, and fix your attention
" on the fecurity of the poffeffions and
" revenues of the Company.' His fuperior
" genius fometimes acted in the fpirit,
" rather than complied with the letter, of
" the law: but he difcharged the truft, and
" preferved the empire committed to his
" care, in the fame way, and with greater
" fplendor and fuccefs than any of his
" predeceffors in office: his departure from
" India was marked with the lamentations
" of the natives and the gratitude of his
countrymen ;

" countrymen ; and on his return to Eng-
" land, he received the cordial congratu-
" lations of that numerous and refpectable
" fociety, whofe interefts he had promoted,
" and whofe dominions he had protected
" and extended."

Gentlemen, if this be a wilfully falfe account
of the inftructions given to Mr. Haftings for his
government, and of his conduct under them, the
author and publifher of this defence deferve the
fevereft punifhment, for a mercenary impofition
on the public. But if it be true that he was directed to make the fafety and profperity of Bengal
the firft object of his attention, and that under
his adminiftration it has been fafe and profperous;
if it be true that the fecurity and prefervation of
our poffeffions and revenues in Afia was marked
out to him as the great leading principle of his
government, and that thefe poffeffions and revenues, amidft unexampled dangers, have been
fecured and preferved ; then a queftion may be
unaccountably mixed with your confideration,
much beyond the confequence of the prefent profecution, involving perhaps the merits of the
impeachment itfelf which gave it birth ; a
queftion which the Commons, as profecutors of
Mr. Haftings, fhould in common prudence have
avoided ; unlefs that, regretting the unwieldy
length of their proceedings againft him, they

wifhed

wifhed to afford him the opportunity of this
ftrange anomolous defence.—For although I am
neither his counfel, nor defire to have any thing to
do with his innocence ; yet in the collateral defence of my client, I am driven to ftate matter
which may be confidered by many as hoftile to
the impeachment. For if our dependencies have
been fecured, and their interefts promoted, I am
driven in the defence of my client to remark, that
it is mad and propofterous to bring to the ftandard
of juftice and humanity, the exercife of a dominion
founded upon violence and terror. It may and
muft be true, that Mr. Haftings has repeatedly
offended againft the rights and privileges of.
Afiatic government, if he was the faithful deputy of a power which could not maintain itfelf
for an hour, without trampling upon both : He
may and muft have offended againft the laws of
God and nature, if he was the faithful viceroy of
an empire wrefted in blood from the people to
whom God and nature had given it : He may and
muft have preferved that unjuft dominion over a
timorous and abject nation, by a terrifying, over-
bearing, infulting fuperiority, if he was the
faithful adminiftrator of your government, which
having no root in confent or affection, no foundation in fimilarity of interefts, nor fupport from
any one principle which cements men together in
fociety, could only be upheld by alternate ftra-
tagem and force. The unhappy people of India,
feeble and effeminate as they are from the foftnefs
of

of their climate, and fubdued and broken as they
have been by the knavery and ftrength of civilization, ftill occafionally ftart up in all the vigour
and intelligence of infulted nature. To be governed at all, they muft be governed with a rod
of iron ; and our empire in the Eaft would over
. and over again have been loft to Great Britain if
civil fkill and military prowefs had not united their
efforts to fupport an authority which heaven never
gave, by means which it never can fanction.

Gentlemen, I think I can obferve that you are
touched with this way of confidering the fubject ;
and I can account for it. I have not been confidering it through the cold medium of books, but
have been fpeaking of man and his nature, and of
human dominion, from what I have feen of them
myfelf amongft reluctant nations fubmitting to our
authority. I know what they feel, and how fuch
feelings can alone be repreffed. I have heard
them in my youth from a naked favage, in the indignant character of a prince furrounded by his
fubjects, addreffing the Governor of a Britifh
colony, holding a bundle of fticks in his
hand, as the notes of his unlettered eloquence.
" Who is it," faid the jealous ruler over the de-
fart encroached upon by the reftlefs foot of
Englifh adventure—" Who is it that caufes this
" river to rife in the high mountains, and to
" empty itfelf into the ocean ? Who is it that
" caufes to blow the loud winds of winter, and
. . G 4   " that

" that calms them again in the summer ? Who is
" it that rears up the shade of these lofty forests,
" and blasts them with the quick lightning at his
" pleasure ? The same being who gave to you a
" country on the other side of the waters, and
" gave our's to us; and by this title we will defend
" it," said the warrior, throwing down his tomo-
hawk upon the ground, and raising the war sound
of his nation. These are the feelings of subju-
gated man all round the globe; and depend upon
it, nothing but fear will controul where it is in vain
to look for affection.

These reflections are the only antidotes to those
anathemas of superhuman eloquence which have
lately shook these walls that surround us; but
which it unaccountably falls to my province, whether I will or no, a little to stem the torrent of; by
reminding you that you have a mighty sway in
Asia, which cannot be maintained by the finer
sympathies of life, or the practice of its charities
and affections : What will they do for you when
surrounded by two hundred thousand men with
artillery, cavalry, and elephants, calling upon you
for their dominions which you have robbed them
of ? Justice may, no doubt, in such a case forbid
the levying of a fine to pay a revolting soldiery :
a treaty may stand in the way of encreasing a tribute to keep up the very existence of the government ; and delicacy for women may forbid all en-
trance into a Zenana for money, whatever may be
the

the neceffity for taking it.—All thefe things muft ever be occurring. But under the preffure of fuch conftant difficulties, fo dangerous to national honour, it might be better perhaps to think of effectually fecuring it altogether, by recalling our troops and our merchants, and abandoning our Oriental empire. Until this is done, neither religion nor philofophy can be preffed very far into the aid of reformation and punifhment. If England, from a luft of ambition and dominion, will infift on maintaining defpotic rule over diftant and hoftile nations, beyond all comparifon more numerous and extended than herfelf, and gives commiffion to her viceroys to govern them with no other inftructions than to preferve them, and to fecure permanently their revenues ; with what colour of confiftency or reafon can fhe place herfelf in the moral chair, and affect to be fhocked at the execution of her own orders; adverting to the exact meafure of wickednefs and injuftice neceffary to their execution, and complaining only of *the excefs as the immorality*, confidering her authority as a difpenfation for breaking the commands of God, and the breach of them as only punifhable when contrary to the ordinances of man.

Gentlemen, fuch a proceeding begets ferious reflections. It would be better perhaps for the mafters and the fervants of all fuch governments, to join in fupplication, that the great author

of

of violated humanity may not confound them together in one common judgment.

Gentlemen, I find, as I faid before, I have not
fufficient ftrength to go on with the remaining
parts of the book. I hope, however, that notwithftanding my omiffions you are now compleatly
fatisfied, that whatever errors or mifconceptions
may have mifled the writer of thefe pages, the juftification of a perfon whom he believed to be innocent, and whofe accufers had appealed to the
public, was the fingle objeƈ of his contemplation.
If I have fucceeded in that objeƈ, every purpofe
which I had in addreffing you has been anfwered.

It only now remains to remind you, that another
confideration has been ftrongly preffed upon you,
and, no doubt, will be infifted on in reply.
—You will be told, that the matters which I
have been juftifying as legal, and even meritorious,
have therefore not been made the fubjeƈ of complaint ; and that whatever intrinfic merit parts of
the book may be fuppofed or even admitted to poffefs, fuch merit can afford no juftification to the
feleƈed paffages, fome of which, even with the
context, carry the meaning charged by the information, and which are indecent animadverfions
on authority.

Gentlemen, to this I would anfwer (ftill pro-
tefting as I do againft the application of any one

of the innuendos,) that if you are firmly perfuaded of the finglenefs and purity of the author's intentions, you are not bound to fubject him to infamy, becaufe, in the zealous career of a juft and animated compofition, he happens to have tripped with his pen into an intemperate expreffion in one or two inftances of a long work. If this fevere duty were binding on your confciences, the liberty of the prefs would be an empty found, and no man could venture to write on any fubject, however pure his purpofe, without an attorney at one elbow, and a counfel at the other.

From minds thus fubdued by the terrors of punifhment, there could iffue no works of genius to expand the empire of human reafon, nor any mafterly compofitions on the general nature of government ; by the help of which, the great commonwealths of mankind have founded their eftablifhments ; much lefs any of thofe ufeful applications of them to critical conjunctures, by which, from time to time, our own conftitution, by the exertion of patriot citizens, has been brought back to its ftandard.

Under fuch terrors, all the great lights of fcience and civilization muft be extinguifhed : for men cannot communicate their free thoughts to one another with a lafh held over their heads.

It

It is the nature of every thing that is great and ufeful, both in the animate and inanimate world, to be wild and irregular; and we muft be contented to take them with their alloys which belong to them or live without them. Genius breaks from the fetters of criticifm, but its wanderings are fanctioned by its majefty and wifdom, when it advances in its path; fubject it to the critic, and you tame it into dulnefs. Mighty rivers break down their banks in the winter, fweeping away to death the flocks which are fattened on the foil that they fertilize in the fummer: The few may be faved by embankments from drowning, but the flock muft perifh for hunger. Tempefts occafionally fhake our dwellings, and diffipate our commerce; but they fcourge before them the lazy elements, which without them would ftagnate into peftilence.

In like manner, Liberty herfelf, the laft and beft gift of God to his creatures, muft be taken juft as fhe is; you may pare her down into bafhful regularity, and fhape her into a perfect model of fevere fcrupulous law, but fhe will be liberty no longer; and you muft be content to die under the lafh of this inexorable juftice which you have exchanged for the banner of freedom.

If it be afked where the line to this indulgence and impunity is to be drawn; the anfwer is eafy.
The

'The liberty of the prefs *on general fubjeɛts* comprehends and implies as much ftriɛt obfervance of pofitive law as is confiftent with perfeɛt purity of intention, and equal and ufeful fociety; and what that latitude is, cannot be promulgated in the abſtraɛt, buṭ muſt be judged of in the particular inſtance, and confequently upon this occafion muſt be judged of by you, without forming any poffible precedent for any other cafe; and where can the judgment be poffibly fo fafe as with the members of that fociety which alone can fuffer if the writing is calculated to do mifchief to the public.

You muſt therefore try the book by that criterion, and fay whether the publication was premature and offenfive, or, in other words, whether the publiſher was bound to have fuppreffed it until the public ear was anticipated and abufed, and every avenue to the human heart or underſtanding fecured and blocked up.

I fee around me thofe, by whom, by and by, Mr. Haſtings will be moſt ably and eloquently defended *; but I am forry to remind my friends,. that but for the right of fufpending the public judgment concerning him till their feafon of exertioń comes round, the tongues of angels would be infufficient for the taſk.

* Mr. Law, Mr. Plumer, and Mr. Dallas.

Gentlemen,

Gentlemen, I hope I have now performed my duty to my client; I sincerely hope that I have; for, certainly, if ever there was a man pulled the other way by his interests and affections,—if ever there was a man who should have trembled at the situation in which I have been placed on this occasion; it is myself, who not only love, honour, and respect, but whose future hopes and preferments are linked from free choice with those who, from the mistakes of the author, are treated with great severity and injustice.——These are strong retardments; but I have been urged on to activity by considerations, which can never be inconsistent with honourable attachments, either in the political or social world; the love of justice and of liberty, and a zeal for the constitution of my country, which is the inheritance of our posterity, of the public, and of the world.

These are the motives which have animated me in defence of this person, who was an entire stranger to me; whose shop I never go to; and the author of whose publication, as well as Mr. Hastings who is the object of it, I never spoke to in my life.

One word more, Gentlemen, and I have done. Every human tribunal ought to take care to administer justice, as we look hereafter to have justice administered to ourselves. Upon the principle which

which the Attorney General prays fentence upon
my client,—God have mercy upon us.—Inftead of
ftanding before him in judgment with the hopes
and confolations of Chriftians, we muft call upon
the mountains to cover us; for which of us can
prefent for omnifcient examination, a pure, un-
fpotted and faultlefs courfe.—But I humbly expect
that the benevolent Author of our being will judge
us as I have been pointing out for your example.
—Holding up the great volume of our lives in his
hands, and regarding the general fcope of them ;
if he difcovers benevolence, charity, and good-
will to man beating in the heart, where he alone
can look;—if he finds that our conduct, though
often forced out of the path by our infirmities, has
been in general well directed ; his all-fearching
eye will affuredly never purfue us into thofe little
corners of our lives, much lefs will his juftice
felect them for punifhment, without the general
context of our exiftence; by which faults may be
fometimes found to have grown out of virtues, and
very many of our heavieft offences to have been
grafted by human imperfection, upon the beft
and kindeft of our affections. No, gentlemen, believe me, this is not the courfe of divine juftice,
or there is no truth in the Gofpels of Heaven.—
If the general tenor of a man's conduct be fuch
as I have reprefented it, he may walk through
the fhadow of death, with all his faults about him,
with as much chearfulnefs as in the common
paths of life; becaufe he knows, that inftead of a
stern

ſtern accuſer to expoſe before the author of his
nature thoſe frail paſſages, which like the ſcored
matter in the book before you chequers the volume of the brighteſt and beſt-ſpent life, his
mercy will obſcure them from the eye of his
purity, and our repentance blot them out for
ever.

All this would I admit be perfectly foreign,
and irrelevant, if you were ſitting here in a caſe
of property between man and man, where a ſtrict
rule of law muſt operate, or there would be an
end in that caſe of civil life and ſociety.

It - would be equally foreign, and ſtill more
irrelevant, if applied to thoſe ſhameful attacks
upon private reputation which are the bane and
diſgrace of the preſs ; by which whole families
have been rendered unhappy during life, by
aſperſions cruel, ſcandalous and unjuſt. *Let*
SUCH LIBELLERS *remember, that no one of my principles of defence can at any time or upon any occaſion
ever apply to ſhield* THEM *from puniſhment ;* becauſe ſuch conduct is not only an infringement
of the rights of men, as they are defined by ſtrict
law, *but is abſolutely incompatible with honor,
honeſty, or miſtaken good intention.*

On ſuch men let the Attorney General bring
forth all the artillery of his office, and the thanks
and bleſſings of the whole public will follow him.
But

But this is a totally different cafe. Whatever private calumny may mark this work, it has not been made the fubject of complaint, and we have therefore nothing to do with that, nor any right to confider it.

We are trying whether the public could have been confidered as offended and endangered, if Mr. Haftings himfelf, in whofe place the author and publifher have a right to put themfelves, had, under all the circumftances which have been confidered, compofed and publifhed the volume under examination. That queftion cannot in common fenfe be any thing refembling *a queftion of* LAW, but is a pure queftion of FACT, to be decided on the principles which I have humbly recommended. I therefore afk of the Court, that the book itfelf may now be delivered to you. Read it with attention, and as you find it pronounce your verdict.

H   REPLY

R E P L Y,

MR. ATTORNEY GENERAL.

Gentlemen of the Jury,

MY learned friend and I ſtand very much contraſted with each other in this cauſe.—To him
belong infinite eloquence, great ingenuity, and
power of perſuaſion, beyond that which I almoſt
ever knew fall to any man's ſhare, and a power
of language greater than that which ever met
my ear.

In his ſituation, it is not only permitted to him,
but it is commendable in him, it is his duty to his
client, to exert all thoſe faculties, to comprehend
every poſſible topic that by the utmoſt ſtretch of
ingenuity can poſſibly be introduced into the moſt
remote connection with this cauſe. I on the
other hand, gentlemen, muſt diſclaim thoſe qua-
lities which I aſcribe to my learned friend—namely,
that ingenuity, that eloquence, and that power of
words ; but if they did belong to me, we ſtand
contraſted alſo in this circumſtance, that I durſt
not in my preſent ſituation uſe them, whatever

little

little effort I might make to that effect in a private
caufe, and acting the part fimply of an advocate—
yet all that I muft abandon, by recollecting the
fituation in which I ftand, which is not that fimply
of an advocate.

Gentlemen, however unworthily, fo it is, that
I ftand in the fituation of, I believe I may fay, the
firft officer of his Lordfhip's Court; therefore the
utmoft plain dealing, the plaineft common fenfe,
and cleareft argument that I can ufe, the utmoft
bona fide's with the Court and Jury, are the duties
incumbent upon me.

In that fpirit therefore, gentlemen, you will not
expect from me the difcharge of my duty, in any
other way than by the moft temperate obfervation,
and by the moft correct and the faireft reafoning
in my power.

One fhould have thought from the general turn
of my learned friend's arguments, that I had in this
information imputed it as a crime to the deceafed
gentleman whom he has named, and whom I
think I hardly recollect ever to have heard named
before, that I had imputed it to him as an offence,
merely that he reafoned in defence of Mr. Haftings
ably and eloquently, as is afferted.

My learned friend has faid, that I have picked
out paffages here and there difconnected and dif-

jointed,

Jointed, and have omitted a vaſt variety of other paſſages. I hardly think that the ſecond obſervation would have been made, had it not been for the ſake of his firſt, but inaſmuch as I ſtudiouſly avoided and would inſert no one ſingle line that conſiſted of fair reaſoning and defence for Mr. Haſtings, inaſmuch as it was no part of my duty ſo to do; he has exculpated me by ſaying, that loading an information with that which was not immediately to the point, was a thing which I avoided with propriety.

This book, as my learned friend himſelf has deſcribed it to you, and read the greater part, conſiſts of many different heads; it conſiſts of an hiſtorical narration of facts, with that I do not quarrel.—It conſiſts of extracts from original papers, with that I do not quarrel.—It conſiſts of arguments, of reaſoning, and of very good declamation, with that I do not quarrel.—But it conſiſts alſo of a ſtain, and a deep ſtain, upon your repreſentatives in Parliament.

My learned friend ſays that this is written with a friendly zeal for Mr. Haſtings. I commend that zeal; but at the ſame time you will permit me to diſtinguiſh, if that could avail, between the zeal of an author for Mr. Haſtings, and the cold lucrative motives of the printer of that author's work. It is the duty of that printer to have that work reviſed by ſome one elſe, if he has not the

capacity

capacity to do it himfelf, to fee that poifon does not circulate among the public. It is his bounden duty to do that; zeal cannot excufe or exculpate the author, much lefs the mechanical printer; though perhaps if this had been fhewn in manufcript as the work of a zealous friend, great allowance might have been made for that zeal.

My learned friend, for the purpofes of argument, deviated into almoft every field that it was poffible for knowledge fuch as his—for reading, experience, knowledge of human nature, and every thing that belongs to it; he has deviated into it at great length, and nine tenths of his argument confifted of it. Inftead of that, what is this queftion —the coldeft, the dulleft, the drieft of all poffible queftions; it is neither more nor lefs than this, Whether when the great tribunal of the nation is carrying on its moft folemn proceeding, for the benefit and for the interefts of the nation, while that is depending, and not yet finally concluded, the accufers, the Houfe of Commons, who carry up their impeachment to the Houfe of Lords, are flandered by being called perfons acting from private and interefted animofity; perfons who ftudioufly, when they find a meritorious fervant of the country come home crowned with laurels, (as it is expreffed,) are fure to do what? To impeach and to ruin him.

H 3I fhall

I shall also studiously avoid any thing respecting politics or party. I shall studiously avoid any thing respecting the conduct of any men in another place; and my learned friend will excuse me also, if I don't state my own.

'These I avoid for this reason, that when we are within these walls, we are to betake ourselves to the true and genuine principles of our law and constitution; it is not that a picture of oppression of one man is to justify the calumniating other men; it will justify the defending that man, but it will not justify a stain upon the House of Commons of this country. And, gentlemen, surely this author, considerable as he is as a man acquainted with composition, betrays himself the cause of Mr. Hastings, as I should think ; at least he does Mr. Hastings no service, by deserting and abandoning the declamation, and the reasoning of which he seems to be a considerable master, and deviating into slander and calumny upon the House of Commons, the accusers of that gentleman.

My learned friend has used an analogy, and he says the House of Commons is a Grand Jury ; I close with him in that analogy ; I ask you, as lovers of good order, as men desirous of repressing licentiousness, as persons who wish that this country should be decently and well governed, whether you would endure for an instant, if this were an information against a defendant, who published
that

that a Grand Jury found that bill, not becaufe they thought it a right thing that the perfon accufed fhould be put upon his trial, but that they found the indictment againft him becaufe he was meritorious, that they did it from principles of private animofity, and not with a regard to public juftice.

If an indictment was brought before you for a flander of that fort upon a Grand Jury, could you hefitate an inftant, in faying that it was reprehenfible, and a thing not to be endured? why then, if the whole reprefentatives of the nation are acting in that capacity, if after many years inveftigation they bring charges againft any individual, is it any apology, juftification it cannot be, for the author of this in his zeal for his friend, to tack to it that which muft be a difgrace to the country if it is true, and therefore muft not be circulated by any perfon whatever.

The commendation which even my learned friend has beftowed upon this work, the paffionate and animated manner in which he has recommended it to your perufal, and that of every man in the country, moft manifeftly proves what I ftated in opening this caufe; which was, that when fuch mifchief as this is in a book, written by a perfon of no mean abilities, it comes recommended to, and in fact mifleads the beft underftandings in the country. I leave any man to judge of what muft

H 4 . be

·be the mifchievous tendency of that, compared
with the fquibs, paragraphs, and idle trafh of the
day, which frequently die away with that day.
Upon this principle certainly it was that thofe
paffages which I feleted and put into this information, and which immediately regard the Houfe
of Commons, naturally gave offence to the
Houfe: they felt themfelves calumniated and af-
perfed, and deferving redrefs from a Jury.

My learned friend fays—Why don't the Houfe
of Commons themfelves punifh it ? Is that an argument to be ufed in the mouth of one who recom-
mends clemency ? Does he recommend the
iron hand of power coming down upon a
man of this fort, and not temperately, wifely,
judicioufly bow to the common law of this country,
and fay let him be dealt with by that common
law?—There he will have a fcrupuloufly impartial
trial ; there he will have every advantage that the
meaneft fubjet of the country is intitled to.

But, fays my learned friend, paffages are feleted
from diftant pages and tacked together ; the context between muft explain the meaning of thofe
paffages ; and he compares it to taking one half of
a fentance, and tells you that if any man fhould
fay, there is no God, taking that part alone, he
would be a blafphemer ; taking the whole verfe,
that the fool hath faid in his heart there is no
God, in that fenfe it becomes diretly the reverfe
of blafphemy—Now has he found any one garbled
fentence

fentence in the whole courfe of this information? Is not every one a clear, diftinct, and feparate propofition?

On the contrary, when he himfelf accufes me, not perfonally but officially, of not having ftated the whole of this volume upon record, and undertaking to fupply my defects, he miffes this very fentence:

" Affertions fo hardy, and accufations fo
" atrocious, ought not to have been in-
" troduced into the preamble of an im-
" peachment, before an affembly fo refpec-
" table as the Houfe of Peers, without the
" cleareft and moft uncontrovertible evi-
" dence. In all tranfactions of a political
" nature there are many concealed move-
" ments that efcape the detection of the
" world; but there are fome facts fo broad
" and glaring, fo confpicuous and pro-
" minent, as to ftrike the general eye, and
" meet the common level of the human
" underftanding."

Now, Gentlemen, I only adduce this to fhew, that it is poffible that two leaves may be turned
over

over at once, on the defendant's fide of the queftion ; and likewife to fhew you that I have not, for
the purpofe of accufation, culled and picked out
every paffage that I might have picked out, or
every one that would bear an offenfive conftruction ; but have taken thofe prominent parts where
this author has abandoned the purpofe my learned
friend afcribes to him, that of extenuating the
guilt imputed to Mr. Haftings, and of fhewing that
he had merit with the public, rather than demerit ;
and to fhew that I have betaken myfelf to the fifth
head of his work, as I enumerated them before,
where he does not content himfelf with executing
that purpofe, but holds out the Houfe of Commons
as perfons actuated by private malice, not only in
the eyes of the fubjects of this country, but alfo to
furrounding nations, whofe eyes are unqueftionably upon this country, throughout the whole
courfe of the proceeding.

I would afk you, whether any reafonable anfwer
has been given to the interpretation, which I put
upon the various paffages in this book?

The firft of them, I admit with my learned friend,
is fimply an introduction ; and is ftated in the information, merely to fhew that the author himfelf knew
the pofition and ftate of things ; that the impeach
ment had been carried up to the Houfe of Lords,
and was there depending for their judgment.

Then

Then, after having reafoned fomewhat upon the introduction to thefe feveral articles of impeach-ment, and after having ftated that thefe had been circulated in India, he goes on to fay,

" Will accufations, built upon fuch a bafelefs
" fabric, prepoffefs the public in favor of
" the impeachment ? What credit can we
" give to multiplied and accumulated
" charges, when we find that they ori-
" ginate from mifreprefentation and falf-
" hood ?"

My learned friend himfelf told you, in a fubfe-quent part of his fpeech, that thofe accufations originated from an inquiry which lafted two years and a half by a Secret Committe of the Houfe of Commons, (of which I myfelf was a pretty labori-ous member ;) if that be fo, what pretence is there here for impregnating the public with a belief, that from falfe, fcandalous and fabricated materi-als, thofe charges did originate ? Is not that giving a directly falfe impreffion to the public from that which is true ? Are not thofe to be protected from flander of this fort, who take fo much pains to in-veftigate what appears to them in the refult to be a fit matter not for them to decide ultimately upon, but to put in a courfe of trial, where ulti-mately juftice will be done.

Has

·- Has my learned friend attempted any explanation, or other interpretation, to be put upon thefe words, than that which the information imputes ?

" If after exerting all your efforts in the caufe
" of your country, you return covered with
" laurels, and crowned with fuccefs; if
" you preferve a loyal attachment to your·
" Sovereign, you may expect the thun-
" ders of parliamentary vengeance ;—you
" will certainly be impeached and proba-
" bly be undone."

Is it to be faid, and circulated in print all over the world, that the Houfe of Commons is compofed of fuch materials that exactly in proportion to a man's merit is their injuftice and inhuman tyranny—Is that to be faid or printed freely, under the pretext that the author is zealous in the intereft of a gentleman under misfortune?

But it is faid there are forty libels every day publifhed againft this gentleman, and no one is permitted to defend him :—Let all mankind defend him :—Let every man that pleafes write what he will, provided he does it within the verge of the law, if he does it as a manly and good fubject, confining himfelf to reafonable and good argument.

My

My learned friend fays, If you ftop this, the
prefs is gagged ; that it never can be faid with impunity, that the King and the conftable are in the
fame predicament.—The King and the conftable
are in one refpect in the fame perdicament, with
infinite difference in the gradition, and an infinite
difference in the comparifon ; but without all queftion, both are magiftrates : the one the higheft, to
whom we look with awe and reverence; but though
of the fame genus, not of the fame fpecies ; that
may be everlaftingly faid in this country, and everlaftingly will be faid.

But is this the way to fecure the liberty of the
prefs, that at the time when the nation is folemnly
engaged in the inveftigation of the conduct of one
of its firft fervants, that that fervant fhould not
only be defended by fair argument and reafon, as
far as it goes, but that his accufers are to be
charged with malice and perfonal animofity againft
that individual ?

If the audacious voice of flander fhould go fo
high as that, who is there that will ever undertake
to be an accufer in this country. I am fure I for
one, who fometimes am called upon (I hope as
fparingly as public exigency will admit of to exercife that odious and difagreeable tafk), would with
pleafure facrifice my gown, if I faw it eftablifhed
that even the higheft accufers that this country
knows are under the pretence of the defence of an

individual

individual to be vilified as thefe accufers are : Can fubordinate accufers expect to efcape ?

Gentlemen, give me leave again to remind you, that nothing can ever fecure a valuable blessing fo effectually as by enforcing the temperate, legal, and difcrete ufe of it ; and it cannot be neceffary for the liberty of the prefs, that it fhould be licentious to fuch an extreme. Believe me, that if this country fhould be worked up, as I expreffed it yefterday, to a paroxyfm of difguft againft the licentioufnefs of the prefs, which has attacked all ranks of men, and now at laft has mounted up to the legiflative body, perhaps it never can be in greater danger ; and fomething may be done in that paroxyfm of difguft that may be the gradual means of fapping the foundation of that beft of our liberties.

Is it not obvious to common fenfe, that if the whole country is rendered indignant by the licentioufnefs of the prefs knowing no bounds, that that is the inftant of its greateft hazard ? Befides, is the folly of the fubjects of Great Britain fuch, that in order to enjoy a thing in all its perfection, and to all its good purpofes, it is neceffary to encourage its extremeft licentioufnefs ? If you do encourage its extremeft licentioufnefs, and this I venture to call fuch, when the great accufatorial body of the nation is flandered in this manner: if you give it that encouragement to day, no man can tell where it will reach this day twelvemonth.

Therefore

Therefore, fo far from cramping the prefs, fo far from fapping its foundation, fo far from doing it an injury ; on the contrary, you are taking the fureft means to preferve it, by diftinguifhing the two parts of this book, and by faying, True it is that any man is at liberty to expound and to explain the conduct of another ; to juftify it if he pleafes in print; by ftating in a manly way that which belongs to his fubject ; but the moment that he fteps afide, and flanders an individual, much more the awful body of the reprefentatives of the people, there he has done wrong ; he has trefpaffed upon the liberty of the prefs, and has imminently hazarded its exiftence as far as in him lay.

Gentlemen, lay your hands upon your hearts, afk yourfelves as men of honour, becaufe I know that binds you as much as your oaths ; afk yourfelves, whether the true meaning of this libel is not, that not from public grounds, not from conviction, not with a view to render public fervice, but from private pique, from private malice, from bye motives, which I call corruption, the House of Commons have been induced to fend this Gentleman to an enquiry before the proper tribunal, and that too as the libel expreffes it, without even reading it, without confideration, without hearing. Judge I fay, whether that be not the true expofition of this libel, and then, Gentlemen, confider with yourfelves what the effect will be, if you ratify and confirm fuch a libel, by fuffering this defendant to efcape.

SUMMING

SUMMING UP.

LORD KENYON.

Gentlemen of the Jury,

I DO not feel that I am called upon to difcufs the nature of this libel, or to ftate to you what the merit of the compofition is, or what the merit of the argument is, but merely to ftate what the queftions are, to which you are to apply your judgment, and the evidence given in fupport of this information.

It is impoffible when one reads the preface to this information, which ftates that the libel was written to afperfe the Houfe of Commons, not to feel that it is a matter of confiderable importance ; for I don't know how far a fixed general opinion that the Houfe of Commons deferves to have crimes imputed to it, may go ; for men that are governed, will be much influenced by the confidence repofed in the governors ; mankind will never forget that governors are not made for the fake of themfelves, but are placed in their refpective ftations, to difcharge the functions of
their

their office for the fake of the public, and if they
fhould ever conceive that the governors are fo
inattentive to their duty, as to exercife their
functions to keep themfelves in power, and for
their own emolument, without attending to the
interefts of the public, government muft be re-
laxed, and at laft crumble to duft; and therefore
if the cafe is made out, which is imputed to the
defendant, it is no doubt a moft momentous cafe
indeed; but though it is fo, it does not follow
that the defendant is guilty; and Juries have been
frequently told, and I am bound in the fituation
in which I ftand, to tell you, that in forming
your judgment upon this cafe, there are two points
for you to attend to, namely :

Whether the defendant, who is charged with
having publifhed this, did publifh it; and

Whether the fenfe which the Attorney General,
by his innuendo's in this information, has affixed
to the different paffages, is fairly affixed to them.

From any confideration as to the firft of thefe
points you are delivered, becaufe it is admitted
that the book was publifhed by the defendant;
but the other is the material point to which you
are to apply your judgment. It has been entered
into with wonderful abilities, much in the detail;
but it is not enough for a man to fay, I am inno-

I   cent;

cent.;—it belongs to the great searcher of hearts to know whether men are innocent or not.; we are to judge of the guilt or innocence of men, (because we have no other rule to go by) by their overt acts, from what they have done.

In applying the innuendos, I accede intirely to what was laid down by the Counsel for the Defendant, and which was admitted yesterday by the Attorney General, as Counsel for the Crown, that you must, upon this information, make up your minds, that this was meant as an aspersion upon the House of Commons—and I admit also, that in forming your opinion, you are not bound to confine your enquiry to those detached passages which the Attorney General has selected as offensive matter, and the subject of prosecution.

But let me on the other side warn you, that though there may be much good writing, good argument, morality and humanity in many parts of it, yet if there are offensive passages, the good part will not sanctify the bad part.

Having stated that, I ought also to tell you, that in order to see what is the sense, to be fairly imputed to those passages that are culled out as the offensive passages, you have a right to look at all the context; you have a right to look at the whole book; and if you find it has been garbled, and that the passages selected by the Attorney General do not bear the sense imputed to them, the man

has

has a right to be acquitted; and God forbid he
fhould be convicted.

It is for you, upon reading the information,
which if you go out of Court you will undoubtedly take with you, comparing it with this pamphlet,.to fee whether the fenfe the Attorney General has affixed, is fairly affixed; always being
guided by this, that where it is truly ambiguous
and doubtful, the inclination of your judgment
fhould be on the fide of innocence ; but if you find
you cannot acquit him without diftorting fentences
you are to meet this cafe, and all other cafes as I
ftated yefterday, with the fortitude of men, feeling
that they have a duty upon them fuperior to all
leaning to parties ; namely, adminiftering juftice
in the particular caufe.

It would be in vain for me to go through this
pamphlet which has been juft put into my hand,
and to fay whether the fenfe affixed is the fair
fenfe or not. As far as difclofed by the information, thefe paffages afford a ftrong bais, that the
fenfe affixed to them is the fair fenfe; but of that you
will judge, not from the paffages themfelves merely,
but by reading the context or the whole book, fo
much at leaft as is neceffary to enable you to afcer-
tain the true meaning of the author.

If I were prepared to comment upon the pamphlet, in my fituation it would be improper for me

to

to do it ; my duty is fulfilled when I point out to you
what the queſtions are that are propoſed to your
judgment, and what the evidence is upon the queſtions ; the reſult is your's and your's only.

The Jury withdrew for about two hours, when
they returned into Court with a Verdict
finding the Defendant

NOT GUILTY.

MR.

Mr. STOCKDALE has fubjoined to the foregoing account of his Trial, the following pages, as the moft comprehenfive, as well as the lateft thing extant, on the fubject of criminal proceedings againft Libels, and the province of the Jury in trying them : a fubject which has long interefted the Public, and been the fubject of frequent controverfy.

The following argument was delivered by Mr. Erfkine, in the Court of King's Bench, on Wednefday, November 15th, 1784, in fupport of an application for a new trial for a fuppofed mifdirection of the Judge, * on the trial of the Dean of St. Afaph, at Shrewfbury; the learned judge's charge to the jury, for the fuppofed error in which the application for a new trial, and the following argument in fupport of it were made, is not inferted : As it was only the

---

* Sir Francis Buller, Bart.

ufual

ufual charge in fimilar cafes, in conformity
to the eftablifhed practice of the Court of
King's Bench, for fome years before,
viz. That the jury were bound to convict
the publifher on proof of the publication,
and of the meaning imputed to it by the innuendos upon the record, however innocent
or even meritorious they might confider the
matter publifhed.

This doctrine, which did not originate with
the great and venerable Earl Mansfield, but
which had been adopted for fome years before
his time, is queftioned by the following argument, as contrary to the more ancient
law of England, and was delivered in reply to
others never publifhed. The doctrines however contained in it were over-ruled by the
judgment of the Court of King's Bench; by
which the confined province of the jury, to the
finding of the publication, and the innuendos,
was again eftablifhed to be law ; the authority
of which Mr. Stockdale does not prefume to
difpute. The arguments however, by which
the contrary opinion may be maintained, have
been

been confidered by many of the greateft lawyers in England to be too important to be
loft; and are the rather preferved by Mr.
Stockdale, as Mr. Erfkine, in his defence on
his late Trial, infifted as formerly; and notwithftanding thefe judgments to the contrary
upon the right of the jury to acquit him upon
what they fhould find refpecting his intention
as publifher, and their opinions of what he
had publifhed *.

* It is worthy of remark, that after the Dean of St.
Afaph had been convicted, on proof of the publication,
according to the doctrine ratified as law by the Court
of King's Bench, which fhut out from both Judge and
Jury at the trial the quality of the thing publifhed, he
was finally and completely difcharged from the profecution, by a motion made by Mr. Erfkine in arreft of judgment. The Court unanimoufly declaring, That no Libel
was ftated on the record. Therefore, upon this principle, a perfon who has publifhed nothing criminal, may
be fubjected to the expence and difgrace of a conviction
by his country; becaufe, as the law ftands, a Judge cannot
give his opinion on the queftion of Libel, or no Libel,
at the trial—we fay cannot, becaufe the opinion of any
particular judge, on this important fubject, cannot be
collected from his directions on a trial for a Libel. For
a judge, until the law be otherwife declared by Parliament, may confider his private judgment as bound by a
feries of high and refpectable decifions.

ARGUMENT

ARGUMENT

THE RIGHTS OF JURIES.

The Hon, T. Erskine.

I AM now to have the honour to addrefs myfelf
to your Lordfhip, in fupport of the rule granted
to me by the Court upon Monday laft, which, as
Mr. Bearcroft has truly faid, and feemed to mark
the obfervation with peculiar emphafis, is a rule
for a new trial. Much of my argument, according to his notion, points another way; whether
its direction be true, or its force adequate to the
object, it is now my bufinefs to fhew.

In rifing to fpeak at this time, I feel all the advantage conferred by the reply over thofe whofe
arguments are to be anfwered; but I feel a difad-
vantage likewife which muft fuggeft itfelf to every
intelligent mind.

In following the objections of fo many learned
perfons, offered in different arrangements upon a
fubject fo complicated and comprehenfive, there
is much danger of being drawn from that method
and order which can alone faften conviction upon
unwilling minds, or drive them from the fhelter
which ingenuity never fails to find in the labyrinth
of a defultory difcourfe.

The

The fenfe of that danger, and my own inability to ftruggle againft it, led me originally to deliver to the court, certain written and maturely confidered propofitions, from the eftablifhment of which I refolved not to depart, or to be removed, either in fubftance or in order, in any ftage of the proceedings, and by which I muft therefore this day unqueftionably ftand or fall.

Purfuing this fyftem I am vulnerable two ways, and in two ways only. Either it muft be fhewn that my propofitions are not valid in law; or admitting their validity, that the learned judge's charge to the jury at Shrewfbury was not repugnant to them: there can be no other poffible objections to my application for a new trial.

My duty to-day is therefore obvious and fimple; it is, firft, to re-maintain thofe propofitions; and then to fhew, that the charge delivered to the jury at Shrewfbury was founded upon the abfolute denial and reprobation of them.

I begin therefore, by faying again in my own original words, that when a bill of indictment is found, or an information filed, charging any crime or mifdemeanor known to the law of England, and the party accufed puts himfelf upon the country by pleading the general iffue, not guilty:— the jury are GENERALLY charged with his deliverance from that CRIME, and not SPECIALLY from the fact or facts, in the commiffion of which the indictment or information charges the crime to confift;

confift; much lefs from any fingle fact, to the exclufion of others charged upon the fame record.

Secondly, That no act which the law in its general theory holds to be criminal, conftitutes in itfelf a crime abftracted from the mifchievous intention of the actor. And that the intention, even where it becomes a fimple inference of legal reafon from a fact or facts eftablifhed, may, and ought to be collected by the jury, with the judge's affiftance. Becaufe the act charged, though eftablifhed as a fact in a trial *on the general iffue*, does not neceffarily and unavoidably eftablifh the criminal intention by any ABSTRACT conclufion of law; the eftablifhment of the fact being ftill no more than full evidence of the crime, but not the crime itfelf; unlefs the jury render it fo themfelves, by referring it voluntarily to the court by fpecial verdict.

Thefe two propofitions, though worded with cautious precifion, and in technical language, to prevent the fubtlety of legal difputation in oppofi-tion to the plain underftanding of the world, neither do nor were intended to convey any other fentiment than this, viz. that in all cafes where the law either directs or permits a perfon accufed of a crime to throw himfelf upon a jury for deliverance, by pleading *generally* that he is not guilty; the jury, thus legally appealed to, may deliver him from the accufation by a general verdict of acquittal (founded as in common-fenfe it evidently muft be) upon an inveftigation as general

and

and comprehenfive as the charge itfelf from which
it is a general deliverance.

· Having faid this, I freely confefs to the Court,
that I am much at a lofs for any further illuftration
of my fubject; becaufe I cannot find any matter
by which it might be further illuftrated, fo clear,
or fo indifputable, either in fact or in law, as the
very propofition itfelf which upon this trial has
been brought into queftion.

Looking back upon the ancient conftitution,
and examining with painful refearch the original
jurifdictions of the country,. I am utterly at a lofs
to imagine from what fources thefe novel limitations of the rights of juries are derived. Even the
bar is not yet trained to the difcipline of maintaining them. My learned friend, Mr. Bearcroft, folemnly abjures them: he repeats to-day what he
avowed at the trial, and is even jealous of the imputation of having meant lefs than he expreffed;
for, when fpeaking this morning of the *right* of the
jury to judge of the whole charge, your lordfhip
corrected his expreffion, by telling him he meant
the *power*, and not the *right*; he caught inftantly
at your words, difavowed your explanation; and,
with a confiftency which does him honour, declared his adherence to his original admiffion in
its full and obvious extent.

" I did not mean," faid he, " merely to ac-
" knowledge that the jury have the *power*; for
" their

" their power nobody ever doubted; and, if a
" judge was to tell them they had it not, they
" would only have to laugh at him, and convince
" him of his error, by finding a general verdict
" which muft be recorded : I meant, therefore, to
" confider it as a *right*, as an important privilege,
" and of great value to the conftitution."

Thus Mr. Bearcroft and I are perfectly agreed;
I never contended for more than he has voluntarily
conceded. I have now his exprefs authority for
repeating, in my own former words, that the jury
have not merely the *power* to acquit, upon a view
of the whole charge, without controul or punifhment, and without the poffibility of their acquittal
being annulled by any other authority; but that
they have *a conftitutional legal right to do it ; a right
fit to be exercifed ;* and intended by the wife foun-
ders of the government, to be a protection to the
lives and liberties of Englifhmen, againft the en-
croachments and perverfions of authority in the
hands of fixed magiftrates.

But this candid admiffion on the part of Mr.
Bearcroft, though very honourable to himfelf, is
of no importance to me, fince, from what has
already fallen from your lordfhip, I am not to expect a ratification of it from the court ; it is therefore my duty to eftablifh it. I feel all the importance of my fubject, and nothing fhall lead me to-
day to go out of it. I claim all the attention of
the

the Court, and the right to ftate every authority which applies in my judgment to the argument, without being fuppofed to introduce them for other purpofes than my duty to my client, and the conftitution of my country warrants and approves.

It is not very ufual, in an Englifh court of juftice, to be driven back to the earlieft hiftory and original elements of the conftitution, in order to eftablifh the firft principles which mark and diftinguifh Englifh law: they are always affumed, and, like axioms in fcience, are made the foundations of reafoning without being proved. Of this fort our anceftors, for many centuries, muft have conceived the right of an Englifh jury to decide upon every queftion which the forms of the law fubmitted to their final decifion; fince, though they have immemorially exercifed that fupreme jurifdiction, we find no trace in any of the ancient books of its ever being brought into queftion.

It is but as yefterday, when compared with the age of the law itfelf, that judges, unwarranted by any former judgments of their predeceffors, without any new commiffion from the Crown, or enlargement of judicial authority from the legiflature, have fought to faften a limitation upon the rights and privileges of jurors, totally unknown in ancient times, and palpably deftructive of the very end and object of their inftitution.

No

No fact, my Lord, is of more eafy demonstra-
tion ; for the hiftory and laws of a free country
lie open even to vulgar infpection.

During the whole Saxon æra, and even long
after the eftablifhment of the Norman government,
the whole adminiftration of juftice, criminal and
civil, was in the hands of the people themfelves,
without the controul or intervention of any judicial
authority, delegated to fixed magiftrates by the
crown. The tenants of every manor adminiftered
civil juftice to one another in the court-baron of
their Lord; and their crimes were judged of in
the leet, every fuitor of the manor giving his
voice as a juror, and the fteward being only the
regifter, and not the judge.

On appeals from thefe domeftic jurifdictions
to the county-court, and to the torn of the fheriff,
or in fuits and profecutions originally commenced
in either of them, the fheriff's authority extended
no further than to fummon the jurors, to compel
their attendance, minifterially to regulate their
proceedings, and to enforce their decifions; and
even where he was fpecially empowered by the
King's writ of *jufticies* to proceed in caufes of
fuperior value, no *judicial* authority was thereby
conferred upon himfelf, but only a more enlarged
jurifdiction ON THE JURORS who were to try the
caufe mentioned in the writ.

It

It is true that the sheriff cannot now inter-meddle in pleas of the crown, but with this exception which brings no restrictions on juries, these jurisdictions remain untouched at this day; intricacies of property have introduced other forms of proceeding, but the constitution is the same.

This popular judicature was not confined to particular districts, or to inferior suits and misdemeanors, but pervaded the whole legal constitution; for, when the Conqueror, to increase the influence of his crown, erected that great superintending court of justice in his own palace, to receive appeals criminal and civil from every court in the kingdom, and placed at the head of it the *Capitalis justicianus totius Angliæ,* of whose original authority the chief justice of this court is but a partial and feeble emanation: even that great magistrate was in the *aula regis* merely ministerial: every one of the king's tenants who owed him service in right of a barony, had a seat and a voice in that high tribunal; and the office of justiciar was but to record and to enforce their judgments.

In the reign of King Edward the First, when this great office was abolished, and the present courts at Westminster established by a distribution of its powers; the barons preserved that supreme superintending jurisdiction which never belonged

to

to the jufticiar, but to themfelves only as the jurors in the king's court: a jurifdiction which, when nobility from being territorial and feodal became perfonal and honorary, was affumed and exercifed by the peers of England, who, without any delegation of judicial authority from the crown, form to this day the fupreme and final court of Englifh law, judging in the laft refort for the whole kingdom, and fitting upon the lives of the peerage, in their ancient and genuine character, as the pares of one another.

When the courts at Weftminfter were eftablifhed in their prefent forms, and when the civilization and commerce of the nation had introduced more intricate queftions of juftice, the judicial authority in civil cafes could not but enlarge its bounds; the rules of property in a cultivated ftate of fociety became by degrees beyond the compafs of the unlettered multitude, and in certain well-known reftrictions undoubtedly fell to the judges; yet more perhaps from neceffity than by confent, as all judicial proceedings were artfully held in the Norman language, to which the people were ftrangers.

Of thefe changes in judicature, immemorial cuftom, and the acquiefcence of the legiflature, is the evidence, which eftablifh the jurifdiction of the courts on the true principles of Englifh law, and meafure the extent of it by their ancient practice.

K   But

But no fuch evidence is to be found of any the leaft relinquifhment or abridgment of popular judicature *in cafes of crimes;* on the contrary, every page of our hiftory is filled with the ftruggles of our anceftors for its prefervation.

The law of property changes with new objects, and becomes intricate as it extends its dominion; but crimes muft ever be of the fame eafy invefti- gation: they confift wholly in intention, and the more they are multiplied by the policy of thofe who govern, the more abfolutely the public free- dom depends upon the people's preferving the entire adminiftration of criminal juftice to them- felves.

In a queftion of property between two private individuals, the crown can have no poffible intereft in preferring the one to the other: but it may have an intereft in crufhing both of them together in defiance of every principle of humanity and juftice, if they fhould put themfelves forward in a contention for public liberty againft a govern- ment feeking to emancipate itfelf from the do- minion of the laws. No man in the leaft ac- quainted with the hiftory of nations, or of his own country, can refufe to acknowledge, that if the adminiftration of criminal juftice were left in the hands of the crown, or its deputies, no greater freedom could poffibly exift than government might choofe to tolerate from the convenience or policy of the day.

My

My Lord, this important truth is no difcovery or affertion of mine, but is to be found in every book of the law : whether we go up to the moft ancient authorities, or appeal to the writings of men of our own times, we meet with it alike in the moft emphatical language. Mr. Juftice Blackftone, by no means biaffed towards demo-cratical government, having, in the third volume of his Commentaries, explained the excellence of the trial by jury in civil cafes, expreffes himfelf thus: vol. 4. p. 349. " But it holds much
" ftronger in criminal cafes; fince in times of
" difficulty and danger, more is to be appre-
" hended from the violence and partiality of
" judges appointed by the crown, in fuits be-
" tween the king and the fubject, than in dif-
" putes between one individual and another, to
" fettle the boundaries of private property. Our
" law has, therefore, wifely placed this ftrong
" and twofold barrier of a prefentment and trial
" by jury, between the liberties of the people
" and the prerogative of the crown: without
" this barrier, juftices of *oyer* and *terminer* named
" by the crown, might, as in France or in
" Turkey, imprifon, difpatch, or exile, any man
" that was obnoxious to government, by an in-
" ftant declaration that fuch was their will and
" pleafure. So that the liberties of England
" cannot but fubfift fo long as this palladium
" remains facred and inviolate, not only from
" all open attacks, which none will be fo hardy

K 2   as

" as to make, but alfo from all fecret machi-
" nations, which may fap and undermine it."

But this remark, though it derives new force
in being adopted by fo great an authority, was
no more original in Mr. Juftice Blackftone than
in me, for the fame exprefs reafon: for the inftitution and authority of juries is to be found
in Bracton, who wrote above five hundred years
before him. " The curia and the pares," fays
he, " were neceffarily the judges in all cafes
" of life, limb, crime and difherifon of the heir
" in capite. The king could not decide, for
" then he would have been both profecutor and
" judge; neither could his juftices, for they re-
" prefent him *."

Notwithftanding all this, the learned judge was
pleafed to fay at the trial, that there was no
difference between civil and criminal cafes. I
fay, on the contrary, independent of thefe authorities, that there is not, even to vulgar obfervation, the remoteft fimilitude between them.

There are four capital diftinctions between
profecutions for crimes, and civil actions, every
one of which deferves confideration.

---

* Vide likewife Mr. Reeves' very ingenious Hiftory of the
Englifh law.

Firft,

First, In the jurifdiction neceffary to found the charge.

Secondly. In the manner of the defendant's pleading to it.

Thirdly, In the authority of the verdict which difcharges him.

Fourthly, In the independence and fecurity of the jury from all confequences in giving it.

As to the firft, it is unneceffary to remind your Lordfhips, that, in a civil cafe, the party who conceives himfelf aggrieved, ftates his complaint to the court, avails himfelf at his own pleafure of its procefs, compels an anfwer from the defendant by its authority, or taking the charge *pro confeffo* againft him on his default, is intitled to final judgment and execution for his debt, without any interpofition of a jury. But in criminal cafes it is otherwife; the court has no cognizance of them, without leave from thé people forming a grand inqueft. If a man were to commit a capital offence in the face of all the judges of England; their united authority could not put him upon his trial: they could file no complaint againft him, even upon the records of the fupreme criminal court; but could only commit him for fafe cuftody, which is equally competent to every common juftice of the peace: the grand jury alone could arraign him, and in their dif-

K 3   cretion

cretion might likewife finally difcharge him, by throwing out the bill, with the names of all your Lordfhips as witneffes on the back of it.

If it fhall be faid, that this exclufive power of the grand jury does not extend to leffer mifdemeanors, which may be profecuted by information; I anfwer, that for that very reafon it be, comes doubly neceffary to preferve the power of the other jury which is left.

But, in the rules of pleading, there is no diftinction between capital and leffer offences; and I venture to affert, that the defendant's plea of not guilty, which univerfally prevails as the legal anfwer to every information or indictment, as oppofed to fpecial pleas to the court in civil actions; and the neceffity impofed upon the crown to join the general iffue, is abfolutely decifive of the prefent queftion,

Every lawyer muft admit, that the rules of pleading were originally eftablifhed to mark and to preferve the diftinct jurifdictions of the court and the jury, by a feparation of the law from the fact wherever they were intended to be feparated. A perfon charged with owing a debt, or having committed a trefpafs, &c. &c. if he could not deny the facts on which the actions were founded, was obliged to fubmit his juftification for matter of law by a fpecial plea to the court upon the record; to which plea the plaintiff might demur, and

and fubmit the legal merits to the judges. By this arrangement, no power was ever given to the jury, by an iffue joined before them, but when a right of decifion, as comprehenfive as the iffue went along with it: for, if a defendant in fuch civil actions pleaded the general iffue inftead of a fpecial plea, aiming at a general deliverance from the charge, by fhewing his juftification to the jury at the trial; the court protected its own-jurifdiction, by refufing all evidence of the facts on which fuch juftification was founded.

The extenfion of the general iffue beyond its ancient limits, and in deviation from its true prin-ciple, has introduced fome confufion into this fimple and harmonious fyftem; but the law is fubftantially the fame.

No man, at this day, in any of thofe actions where the ancient forms of our jurifprudence are ftill wifely preferved, can poffibly get at the opinion of a jury upon any queftion not intended by the conftitution for their decifion. In actions of debt, detinue, breach of covenant, trefpafs, or replevin, the defendant can only fubmit the mere fact to the jury; the law muft be pleaded to the court: if, dreading the opinion of the judges, he conceals his juftification under the cover of a general plea in hopes of a more favourable con-ftruction of his defence at the trial; its very ex-iftence can never even come within the knowledge of the jurors; every legal defence muft arife out of

facts,

facts, and the authority of the judge is interpofed, to prevent their appearing before a tribunal which, in fuch cafes, has no competent jurifdiction over them.

By impofing this neceffity of pleading every legal juftification to the court, and by this exclufion of all evidence on the trial beyond the negation of the fact, the courts indifputably intended to eftablifh, and did in fact effectually fecure the judicial authority over legal queftions from all encroachment or violation; and it is impoffible to find a reafon in law, or in commonfenfe, why the fame boundaries between the fact and the law fhould not have been at the fame time extended to criminal cafes by the fame rules of pleading, if the jurifdiction of the jury had been defigned to be limited to the fact as in civil actions.

But no fuch boundary was ever made or attempted ; on the contrary, every perfon charged with any crime by an indictment or information, has been in all times from the Norman conqueft to this hour, not only permitted, but even bound to throw himfelf upon his country for deliverance, by the general plea of not guilty ; and may fubmit his whole defence to the jury, whether it be a negation of the fact, or a juftification of it in law : and the judge has no authority as in a civil cafe, to refufe fuch evidence at the trial, as out of the iffue, and as *coram non judice*, an authority

rity which in common fenfe he certainly would
have, if the jury had no higher jurifdiction in the
one cafe than in the other. The general plea
thus fanctioned by immemorial cuftom, fo blends
the law and the fact together, as to be infeparable
but by the voluntary act of the jury in finding a
fpecial verdict: the general inveftigation of the
whole charge is therefore before them, and although the defendant admits the fact laid in
the information or indictment, he, neverthelefs,
under his general plea, gives evidence of others
which are collateral, referring them to the judgment of the jury, as a legal excufe or juftification,
and receives from their verdict a compleat, general, and conclufive deliverance.

Mr. Juftice Blackftone, in the fourth volume
of his Commentaries, page 339, fays, " The
" traiterous or felonious intent are the points
" and very gift of the indictment, and muft be
" anfwered directly by the general negative, not
" guilty, and the jury will take notice of any
" defenfive matter, and give their verdict ac-
" cordingly, as effectually as if it were fpecially
" pleaded."

This, therefore, fays Sir Matthew Hale, in his
Pleas of the Crown, page 258, is, upon all ac-
counts, the moft advantageous plea for the defendant: " It would be a moft unhappy cafe for
" the judge himfelf if the prifoner's fate depended
" upon his directions; unhappy alfo for the
                              " prifoner:

" prifoner: for if the judge's opinion muft
" rule the verdict, the trial by jury would be
" ufelefs."

My Lord, the conclufive operation of the verdict when given, and the fecurity of the jury
from all confequences in giving it, renders the
contraft between criminal and civil cafes ftriking
and compleat. No new trial can be granted as
in a civil action: your Lordfhips, however you
may difapprove of the acquittal, have no authority to award one; for there is no precedent of
any fuch upon record, and the difcretion of the
court is circumfcribed by the law.

Neither can the jurors be attainted by the
crown. In Bufhel's cafe, Vaughan's Reports,
page 146, that learned and excellent judge expreffed himfelf thus: " There is no cafe in all
" the law of an attaint for the king, nor any
" opinion but that of Thyrning's, 10th of Henry
" IVth, title Attaint, 60 and 64, for which there
" is no warrant in law, though there be other
" fpecious authority againft it, touched by none
" that have argued this cafe."

Lord Mansfield. To be fure it is fo.

Mr. Erfkine. Since that is clear, my Lord,
I fhall not trouble the court farther upon it:
indeed I have not been able to find any one
authority for fuch an attaint but a dictum in
Fitz-

Fitzherbert's Natura Brevium, page 107; and on the other hand, the doctrine of Bushel's case is expresly agreed to in very modern times, vide Lord Raymond's Reports, 1st volume, page 469.

If then your Lordships reflect but for a moment upon this comparative view of criminal and civil cases which I have laid before you; how can it be seriously contended, not merely that there is no difference, but that there is any the remotest similarity between them. In the one-case, the power of accusation begins from the court; in the other, from the people only, forming a grand jury. In the one, the defendant must plead a special justification, the merits of which can only be decided by the judges; in the other, he may throw himself for general deliverance upon his country. In the first the court may award a new trial if the verdict for the defendant be contrary to the evidence or the law; in the last, it is conclusive and unalterable; and to crown the whole, the King never had that process of attaint which belonged to the meanest of his subjects.

When these things are attentively considered, I might ask those who are still disposed to deny the right of the jury to investigate the whole charge, whether such a solecism can be conceived to exist in any human government; much less in the most refined and exalted in the world; as
that

that a power of fupreme judicature fhould be conferred at random by the blind forms of the law
where no right was intended to pafs with it, and
which was upon no occafion and under no circum-
ftance to be exercifed; which, though exerted
notwithftanding in every age and in a thoufand inftances, to the confufion and difcomfiture of fixed
magiftracy, fhould never be checked by authority,
but fhould continue on from century to century,
the revered guardian of liberty and of life, arreft-
ing the arm of the moft headftrong government in
the worft of times, without any power in the crown
or its judges, to touch without its confent the
meaneft wretch in the kingdom, or even to 'afk
the reafon and principle of the verdict which ac-
quits him. That fuch a fyftem fhould prevail in
a country like England, without either the original inftitution or the acquiefcing fanction of the
legiflature is impoffible. Believe me, my Lord,
no talents can reconcile, no authority can fanction
fuch an abfurdity; the common fenfe of the world
revolts at it.

Having eftablifhed this important right in the jury
beyond all poffibility of cavil or controverfy, I will
now fhew your Lordfhip that its exiftence is not
merely confiftent with theory, but is illuftrated and
confirmed by the univerfal practice of all judges; not
even excepting Mr. Juftice Forfter himfelf, whofe
writings have been cited in fupport of the contrary
opinion. How a man expreffes his abftract ideas
is but of little importance when an appeal can be
made

made to his plain directions to others, and to his own particular conduct: but even none of his expreſſions when properly conſidered and underſtood militate againſt my poſition.

In his juſtly celebrated book on the criminal law, page 256, he expreſſes himſelf thus: " The " conſtruction which the law putteth upon fact " STATED AND AGREED OR FOUND by a jury, *is* " *in all caſes undoubtedly the proper province of the* " *court.*"

Now if the adverſary is diſpoſed to ſtop here, though the author never intended he ſhould, as is evident from the reſt of the ſentence, yet I am willing to ſtop with him, and to take it as a ſubſtantive propoſition; for the ſlighteſt attention muſt diſcover that it is not repugnant to any thing which I have ſaid. Facts *ſtated and agreed*, or facts *found* by a jury, which amounts to the ſame thing, conſtitute a ſpecial verdict; and who ever ſuppoſed that the law upon a ſpecial verdict was not the province of the court? Who ever denied, that where upon a general iſſue the parties chuſe to agree upon facts and to ſtate them; or the jury chuſe voluntarily to find them without drawing the legal concluſion themſelves, that in ſuch inſtances the court is to draw it? That Forſter meant nothing more than that the court was to judge of the law when the jury thus voluntarily prays its aſſiſtance by ſpecial verdict, is evident from his words which follow, for he immediately goes on to ſay; in caſes of doubt and REAL difficulty, it is therefore commonly recommended to the jury

to ſtate faᶜts and circumſtances in a ſpecial verdiᶜt: but neither here, nor in any other part of
his works, is it ſaid or infinuated that they are
bound to do ſo but at their own free diſcretion:
indeed, the very term *recommended*, admits the
contrary, and requires no commentary. I am
ſure I ſhall never diſpute the wiſdom or expediency of ſuch a recommendation in thoſe caſes of
doubt, becauſe the more I am contending for the
exiſtence of ſuch an important right, the leſs it
would become me to be the advocate of raſhneſs
and precipitation in the exerciſe of it.

It is no denial of juriſdiᶜtion to tell the greateſt
magiſtrate upon earth to take good counſel in caſes
of real doubt and difficulty. Judges upon trials,
whoſe authority to ſtate the law is indiſputable,
often refer it to be more ſolemnly argued before
the court; and this court itſelf often holds a meet-
ing of the twelve judges before it decides on a
point upon its own records, of which the others
have confeſſedly no cognizance till it comes before
them by the writ of error of one of the parties.—
Theſe inſtances are monuments of wiſdom, inte-
grity, and diſcretion, but they do not bear in the
remoteſt degree upon juriſdiᶜtion: the ſphere of
juriſdiᶜtion is meaſured by what may or may not
be decided by any given tribunal with legal effeᶜt,
not by the reᶜtitude or error of the deciſion. If the
jury according to theſe authorities may determine
the whole matter by their verdiᶜt, and if the verdiᶜt when given is not only final and unalterable,
but muſt be enforced by the authority of the
judges,

judges, and executed if refifted by the whole power of the ftate; upon what principle of government or reafon can it be argued not to be law? that the jury are in this exact predicament is confeffed by Forfter; for he concludes with faying, that when the law is clear, the jury under the direction of the court in point of law *may*, and if they are well advifed will, *always find a general verdict conformably to fuch directions.*

' This is likewife. confiftent with my pofition: if the law be clear, we may prefume that the judge ftates it clearly to the jury; and if he does, undoubtedly the jury, if they are well advifed, will find according to fuch directions; for they have not a capricious difcretion to make law at their pleafure, but are bound in confcience as well as judges are to find it truly; and generally fpeaking, the learning of the judge who prefides at the trial affords them a fafe fupport and direction.

The fame practice of judges in ftating the law to the jury, as applied to the particular cafe before them, appears likewife in the cafe of the King againft Oneby, 2d Lord Raymond, page 1494. " On the trial the judge directs the jury thus: If you believe fuch and fuch witneffes who have fworn to fuch and fuch facts, *the killing of the deceafed appears to be with malice prepenfe:* but if you do not believe them, then you ought to find him guilty of manflaughter; and the jury may,

may, if they think proper, give a general verdict of murder or manſlaughter : *but if they decline* giving a general verdict, and *will* find the facts ſpecially, the court is then to form their judgment from the facts found, whether the defendant be guilty or not guilty, *i. e.* whether the act was done with malice and deliberation or not."

Surely language can expreſs nothing more plainly or unequivocally, than that where the general iſſue is pleaded to an indictment, the law and the fact are both before the jury ; and that the former can never be ſeparated from the latter, for the judgment of the court, unleſs by their own ſpontaneous act : for the words are, " If " they decline giving a general verdict, and *will* " find the facts ſpecially, the court is THEN to " form their judgment from the facts found." So that after a general iſſue joined, the authority of the court only commences when the jury chooſes to decline the deciſion of the law by a general verdict ; the right of declining which legal determination, is by-the-by a privilege conferred on them by the ſtatute of Weſtminſter, 2d, and by no means a reſtriction of their powers.

But another very important view of the ſubject remains behind : for ſuppoſing I had failed in eſtabliſhing that contraſt between criminal and civil caſes, which is now too clear not only to to require, but even to juftify another obfervation, the argument would lofe nothing by the failure; the fimilarity between criminal and civil cafes derives all its application to the argument from the learned judge's fuppofition, that the jurifdiction of the jury over the law was never contended for in the latter, and confequently on a principle of equality could not be fupported in the former; whereas, I do contend for it, and can inconteftibly eftablifh it in both. This application of the argument is plain from the words of the charge: " If the jury could find the law, it would " undoubtedly hold in civil cafes as well as cri- " minal: but was it ever fuppofed that a jury " was competent to fay the operation of a fine, " or a recovery, or a warranty, which are mere " queftions of law?"

To this queftion I anfwer, that the competency of the jury in fuch cafes is contended for to the full extent of my principle, both by Lyttleton and by Coke: they cannot indeed decide upon them, *de plano*, which, as Vaughan truly fays, is unintelligible, becaufe an unmixed queftion of law can by no poffibility come before them for decifion; but whenever (which very often happens) the operation of a fine, a recovery, a warranty, or any other record or conveyance known to the law of England comes forward, mixed with the fact on the general iffue, the jury have then moft unqueftionably a right to determine it; and what is more, no other autho-

L   rity

rity poffibly can; becaufe when the general iffue is permitted by law, thefe queftions cannot appear on the record for the judgment of the court, and although it can grant a new trial, yet the fame queftion muft ultimately be determined by another jury. This is not only felf-evident to every lawyer, but, as I faid, is exprefsly laid down by Lyttleton in the 368th fection. " Alfo in fuch " cafe where the inqueft may give their verdict " at large, if they will take upon them the " knowledge of the law upon the mat- " ter, they may give their verdict generally " as it is put in their charge: as in the cafe " aforefaid they may well fay, that the leffor did " not diffeife the leffee if they will." Coke, in his commentary on this fection, confirms Lyt- tleton, faying, That in doubtful cafes they fhould find fpecially for fear of an attaint; and it is plain that the ftatute of Weftminfter the 2d, was made either to give or to confirm the right of the jury to find the matter fpecially if they would, leaving their jurifdiction over the law as it ftood by the common law. The words of the ftatute of Weftminfter 2d, chapter 30th, are, " Ordinatum eft quod jufticiarii ad affizas capi- " endias affignati, non compellant juratores dicere " precife fi fit deffina vel non ; dummodo dicere " voluerint veritatem facti et petere auxilium. " curiœ."

From thefe words it fhould appear, that the jurifdiction of the jury over the law when it came
before.

before them on the general iffue, was fo vefted in them by the conftitution, that the exercife of it in all cafes had been confidered to be compulfory upon them, and that this act was a legiflative relief from that compulfion in the cafe of an affize of diffeizin: it is equally plain from the remaining words of the act, that their jurifdiction remained as before ; " fed fi fponte velent diciere " quod diffeifina eft vel non, admittatur eorum " veredictum fub fuo periculo."

But the moft material obfervation upon this ftatute as applicable to the prefent fubject is, That the terror of the attaint from which it was paffed to relieve them, having (as has been fhewn) no exiftence in cafes of crime, the act only extended to relieve the jury at their difcretion from finding the law in civil actions; and confequently it is only from cuftom, and not from pofitive law, that they are not *even compellible* to give a general verdict involving a judgment of law on every criminal trial.

Thefe principles and authorities certainly eftablifh that it is the duty of the judge on every trial where the general iffue is pleaded, to give to the jury his opinion on the law as applied to the cafe before them; and that they muft find a general verdict comprehending a judgment of law, unlefs they choofe to refer it fpecially to the court.

But

But we are here, in a cafe where it is contended, that the duty of the judge is the direct contrary of this: that he is to give no
opinion at all to the jury upon the law as applied
to the cafe before them; that they likewife are
to refrain from all confideration of it, and yet
that the very fame general verdict comprehending
both fact and law, is to be given by them
as if the whole legal matter had been fummed
up by the one and found by the other.

I confefs I have no organs to comprehend the
principle on which fuch a practice proceeds.
I contended for nothing more at the trial than
the very practice recommended by Forfter and
Lord Raymond : I addreffed myfelf to the jury
upon the law with all poffible refpect and de-
ference, and indeed with very marked perfonal
attention to the learned judge: fo far from
urging the jury dogmatically to think for themfelves without his conftitutional affiftance, I called
for his opinion on the queftion of libel, faying,
'That if he fhould tell them diftinctly the paper
indicted was libellous, though I fhould not admit
that they were bound at all events to give effect
to it if they felt it to be innocent ; yet I was
ready to agree that they ought not to go againft
the charge without great confideration : but that
if he fhould fhut himfelf up in filence, giving
no opinion at all upon the criminality of the
paper from which alone any guilt could be faf-
tened on the publifher, and fhould narrow their

con-

confideration to the publication, I entered my protest against their finding a verdict affixing the epithet of *guilty* to the mere fact of publishing a paper, the guilt of which they had not investigated.

If, after this addrefs to the jury, the learned judge had told them, that in his opinion the paper was a libel, but still leaving it to their judgments, and leaving likewife the defendant's evidence to their confideration, had further told them, that he thought it did not exculpate the publication; and if, in confequence of fuch directions, the jury had found a verdict for the crown, I fhould never have made my prefent motion for a new trial: becaufe I fhould have confidered fuch a verdict of guilty as founded upon the opinion of the jury on the whole matter as left to their confideration, and muft have fought my remedy by arreft of judgment on the record.

But the learned judge took a direct contrary courfe: he gave no opinion at all on the guilt or innocence of the paper; he took no notice of the defendant's evidence of intention; told the jury, in the moft explicit terms, that neither the one nor the other were within their jurifdiction; and upon the mere fact of publication directed a general verdict comprehending the epithet of guilty, after having exprefsly withdrawn from the jury every confideration of the merits of the

paper

paper publifhed, or the intention of the publifher, from which it is admitted on all hands the guilt of publication could alone have any ex. iftence.

My motion is therefore founded upon this ob-vious and fimple principle; that the defendant has had in fact no trial ; having been found guilty without any inveftigation of his guilt, and without any power left to the jury to take cog-nizance of his innocence. I undertake to fhew, that the jury could not poffibly conceive or believe from the judge's charge, that they had any jurifdiction to acquit him, however they might have been impreffed even with the merit of the publication, or convinced of his meritorious intention in publifhing it : nay, what is worfe, while the learned judge totally deprived them of their whole jurifdiction over the queftion of libel and the defendant's feditious intention, he at the fame time directed a general verdict of guilty, which comprehended a judgment upon both.

When I put this conftruction on the learned judge's direction, I found myfelf wholly on the language in which it was communicated ; and it will be no anfwer to fuch conftruction, that no fuch reftraint was meant to be conveyed by it. If the learned judge's intentions were even the direct contrary of his expreffions, yet if in con-fequence of that which was expreffed though

not

not intended, the jury were abridged of a jurif-diction which belonged to them by law, and in the exercife of which the defendant had an in-tereft, he is equally a fufferer, and the verdict given under fuch mifconception of authority is equally void: my application ought therefore to ftand or fall by the charge itfelf, upon which I difclaim all difingenuous cavilling. I am cer-tainly bound to fhew, that from the general refult of it, fairly and liberally interpreted, the jury could not conceive that they had any right to extend their confideration beyond the bare fact of publication, fo as to acquit the defendant by a judgment founded on the legality of the dialogue, or the honefty of the intention in pub-lifhing it.

In order to underftand the learned judge's direction, it muft be recollected that it was ad-dreffed to them in anfwer to me, who had con-tended for nothing more than that thefe two confiderations ought to rule the verdict; and it will be feen, that the charge, on the contrary, not only excluded both of them by general in-ference, but by expreffions, arguments, and illuf-trations the moft ftudioufly felected to convey that exclufion, and to render it binding on the con-fciences of the jury.

After telling them in the very beginning of his charge, that the fingle queftion for their decifion was, Whether the defendant had pub-

lifhed

lifhed the pamphlet? he declared to them, that it was not even *allowed* to him, as the judge trying the caufe, to fay whether it was or was not a libel: for that if he fhould fay it was no libel, and they following his direction fhould acquit the defendant; they would thereby deprive the profecutor of his writ of error upon the record, which was one of his deareft birthrights. The law, he faid, was equal between the profecutor and the defendant; that a verdict of acquittal would clofe the matter for ever, depriving him of his appeal; and that whatever therefore was upon the record *was not for their decifion*, but might be carried at the pleafure of either party to the Houfe of Lords.

Surely language could not convey a limitation upon the right of the jury over the queftion of libel, or the intention of the publifher, more pofitive or more univerfal. It was pofitive, inafmuch as it held out to them that fuch a jurifdiction could not be entertained without injuftice; and it was univerfal becaufe the principle had no fpecial application to the particular circumftances of that trial; but fubjected every defendant upon every profecution for a libel, to an inevitable conviction on the mere proof of publifhing *any thing*, though both judge and jury might be convinced that the thing publifhed was innocent and even meritorious.

My.

My Lord, I make this commentary without the hazard of contradiction from any man whose reason is not disordered. For if the prosecutor in every case has a birthright by law to have the question of libel left open upon the record, which it can only be by a verdict of conviction on the single fact of publishing; no legal right can at the same time exist in the jury to shut out that question by a verdict of acquittal founded upon the merits of the publication, or the innocent mind of the publisher.

Rights that are repugnant and contradictory cannot be co-existent. The jury can never have a constitutional right to do an act beneficial to the defendant, which when done deprives the prosecutor of a right which the same constitution has vested in him. No right can belong to one person, the exercise of which in every instance must necessarily work a wrong to another. If the prosecutor of a libel has in every instance the privilege to try the merits of his prosecution before the judges, the jury can have no right in any instance to preclude his appeal to them by a general verdict for the defendant.

The jury therefore from this part of the charge must necessarily have felt themselves absolutely limited (I might say even in their powers) to the fact of publication; because the highest re-straint upon good men is to convince them that they cannot break loose from it without injustice:
and

and the power of a good citizen is never more effectually deftroyed than when he is made to believe that the exercife of it will be a breach of his duty to the public, and a violation of the laws of his country.

But fince equal juftice between the profecutor and the defendant is the pretence for this abridgment of jurifdiction, let us examine a little how it is effected by it.

Do the profecutor and the defendant really ftand upon an equal footing by this mode of proceeding? with what decency this can be alledged, I leave thofe to anfwer who know that it is only by the indulgence of Mr. Bearcroft, of counfel for the profecution, that my reverend client is not at this moment in prifon *, while we are difcuffing this notable equality.

Befides, my Lord, the judgment of this court, though not final in the conftitution, and therefore not binding on the profecutor, is abfolutely conclufive on the defendant. If your Lordfhips pronounce the record to contain no libel, and arreft the judgment on the verdict, the profecutor may carry it to the Houfe of Lords; and pending his

---

* Lord Mansfield ordered the Dean to be committed on the motion for the new trial, and faid, he had no difcretion to fuffer him to be at large, without confent, after his appearance in court, on conviction. Upon which, Mr. Bearcroft gave his confent that the Dean fhould remain at large upon bail.

writ

writ of error remains untouched by your Lordſhip's deciſion. But, if judgment be againſt the
defendant, it is only at the diſcretion of the crown
(as it is ſaid) and not of right, that he can pro-
ſecute any writ of error at all; and even if he
finds no obſtruction in that quarter, it is but at
the beſt an appeal for the benefit of public liberty, from which he himſelf can have no perſonal benefit; for the writ of error being no ſu-
perſedeas, the puniſhment is inflicted on him in
the mean time.

In the caſe of Mr. Horne, this court impri-
ſoned him for publiſhing a libel upon its own
judgment, pending his appeal from its juſtice;
and he had ſuffered the utmoſt rigour which the
law impoſed upon him as a criminal, at the time
that the Houſe of Lords, with the aſſiſtance of
the twelve judges of England, were gravely aſſembled to determine, whether he had been
guilty of any crime. I do not mention this caſe
as hard or rigorous on Mr. Horne, as an individual: it is the general courſe of practice, but
ſurely that practice ought to put an end to this
argument of equality between proſecutor and pri-
ſoner.

It is adding inſult to injury, to tell an innocent
man who is in a dungeon pending his writ of
error, and of whoſe innocence, both judge and
jury were convinced at the trial; that he is in
equal ſcales with his proſecutor, who is at large,

becauſe

becaufe he has an opportunity of deciding after, the expiration of his punifhment, that the profecution had been unfounded, and his fufferings unjuft.

By parity of reafoning, a prifoner in a capital cafe is to be hanged in the mean time for the benefit of equal juftice; leaving his executors to fight the battle out with his profecutor upon the record, through every court in the kingdom: by which at laft his attainder muft be reverfed, and the blood of his pofterity remain uncorrupted. What juftice can be more impartial or equal!

So much for this right of the profecutor of a libel to *compel* a jury in every cafe, generally to convict a defendant on the fact of publication, or to find a fpecial verdict. A right unheard of before fince the birth of the conftitution; not even founded upon any equality in fact, even if fuch a fhocking parity could exift in law, and not even contended to exift in any other cafe where private men become the profecutors of crimes for the ends of public juftice.

It can have, generally fpeaking, no exiftence in any profecution for felony; becaufe the general defcription of the crime in fuch indictments, for the moft part, fhuts out the legal queftion. in the particular inftance, from appearing on the record: and for the fame reafon, it can have no place, even in appeals of death, &c. the only

cafes

cafes where profecutors appear as the revengers of their own private wrongs, and not as the reprefentatives of the crown.

The learned judge proceeded next to eftablifh the fame univerfal limitation upon the power of the Jury, from the hiftory of different trials, and the practice of former judges who prefided at them. And while I am complaining of what I conceive to be injuftice, I muft take care not to be unjuft myfelf. I certainly do not, nor ever did confider the learned judge's mifdirection in his charge to be peculiar to himfelf: it was only the refiftance of the defendant's evidence, and what paffed after the jury returned into court with the verdict, that I ever confidered to be a departure from all precedents : the reft had undoubtedly the fanction of feveral modern cafes; and I wifh, therefore, to be diftinctly underftood, that I partly found my motion for a new trial in oppofition to thefe decifions. It is my duty to fpeak with deference of all the judgments of this court; and I feel an additional refpect for fome of thofe I am about to combat, becaufe they are your Lordfhip's : but comparing them with the judgments of your predeceffors for ages, which is the higheft evidence of Englifh law, I muft be forgiven if I prefume to queftion their authority.

My Lord, it is neceffary that I fhould take notice of fome of them as they occur in the learned judge's judge's charge; for although he is not refponfible for the rectitude of thofe precedents which he only cited in fupport of it, yet the defendant is unqueftionably entitled to a new trial, if their principles are not ratified by the court: for whenever the learned judge cited precedents to warrant the limitation on the province of the jury impofed by his own authority, it was fuch an adoption of the doctrines they contained, as made them a rule to the jury in their decifion.

First then, the learned judge, to overturn my argument with the jury for their jurifdiction over the whole charge, oppofed your Lordfhip's eftablifhed practice for eight and twenty years; and the weight of this great authority was encreafed by the general manner in which it was ftated; for I find no expreffions of your Lordfhip's in any of the reported cafes which go the length contended for. I find the practice, indeed, fully warranted by them; but I do not meet with the principle which can alone vindicate that practice, fairly and diftinctly avowed. The learned judge, therefore, referred to the charge of chief juftice Raymond, in the cafe of the King and Franklin, in which the univerfal limitation contended for, is indeed laid down, not only in the moft unequivocal ' expreffions, but the ancient jurifdiction of juries, refting upon all the authorities I have cited, treated as a ridiculous notion which had been juft taken up a little before the year 1731; and which

no

no man living had ever dreamt of before. The learned judge obferved, that Lord Raymond ftated to the jury on Franklin's trial, that there were three queftions : the firft was, the faƈt of publifhing the Craftfman. Secondly, whether the averments in the information were true : but that the third, viz. whether it was a libel, was merely a queftion of *law* with which the jury *had nothing to do,* as had been then of late thought by fome people who ought to have known better.

This direƈtion of Lord Raymond's was fully ratified and adopted in all its extent, and given to the jury, on the prefent trial, with feveral others of the fame import, as an unerring guide for their conduƈt ; and furely human ingenuity could not frame a more abftraƈt and univerfal limitation upon their right to acquit the defendant by a general verdiƈt ; for Lord Raymond's expreffions amount to an abfolute denial of the right of the jury to find the defendant not guilty, if the publication and innuendos are proved. " Libel or no " libel, is a queftion of law with which you, the " jury, *have nothing to do.*" How then can they have any right to give a general verdiƈt confiftently with this declaration ? can any man in his fenfes colleƈt that he has a right to decide on that with which he has nothing to do ?

But it is needlefs to comment on thefe expreffions, for the jury were likewife told by the learned

judge

judge himſelf, that if they believed the fact of publication, they were *bound* to find the defendant
guilty; and it will hardly be contended, that a
man has a right to refrain from doing that which
he is bound to do.

Mr. Cowper, as counſel for the proſecution, took
upon him to explain what was meant by this expreſſion; and I ſeek for no other conſtruction:
" The learned judge (ſaid he) did not mean to
" deny the right of the jury, but only to convey,
" that there was a religious and moral obligation
" upon them to refrain from the exerciſe of it."

Now, if the principle which impoſed that obligation had been alledged to be ſpecial, applying only to the particular caſe of the Dean of
St. Aſaph, and conſequently conſiſtent with the
right of the jury, to a more enlarged juriſdiction
in other inſtances: telling the jury that they were
bound to convict on proof of publication, might be
plauſibly conſtrued into a recommendation to refrain from the exerciſe of their right in that caſe,
and not to a general denial of its exiſtence: but the
moment it is recollected, that the principle which
bound them was not particular to the inſtance,
but abſtract, and univerſal, binding alike in every
proſecution for a libel, it requires no logic to pronounce the expreſſion to be an abſolute, unequivocal, and univerſal denial of the right: common
ſenſe tells every man, that to ſpeak of a perſon's
right

right to do a thing which yet in every poſſible inſtance where it might be exerted, he is religiouſly
and morally bound not to exert, is not even
ſophiſtry, but downright vulgar nonſenſe.

But, my Lord, the jury were not only limited
by theſe modern precedents, which certainly have
an exiſtence; but were in my mind limited with
ſtill greater effečt by the learned judge's declaration, that ſome of thoſe antient authorities on
which I had principally relied for the eſtabliſhment
of their juriſdičtion, had not merely been over-
ruled, but were altogether inapplicable. I particularly obſerved how much ground I loſt with the
jury, when they were told from the bench, that
even in Buſhel's caſe, on which I had ſo greatly
depended, the very reverſe of my dočtrine had
been expreſsly eſtabliſhed : The court having ſaid
unanimouſly in that caſe, according to the learned
judge's ſtate of it, that if the jury be aſked what
the law is, they cannot ſay, and having likewiſe ratified in expreſs terms the maxim, *Ad queſtionem legis non reſpondent juratores.*

My Lord, this declaration from the bench,
which I confeſs not a little ſtaggered and ſurprized
me, rendered it my duty to look again into
Vaughan, where Buſhel's caſe is reported; I have
performed that duty, and now take upon me po-
ſitively to ſay, that the words of Lord Chief
Juſtice Vaughan, which the learned judge con-
M   ſidered

fidered as a judgment of the court, denying the jurifdiction of the jury over the law, *where a ge-neral iffue is joined before them*, were on the contrary made ufe of by that learned and excellent perfon, to expofe the fallacy of fuch a mifapplication of the maxim alluded to, by the counfel againft Bufhel; declaring that it had no reference' to any cafe where the law and the fact were incorporated by the plea of not guilty, and confirming the right of the jury to find the law upon every fuch iffue, in terms the moft emphatical and expreffive. This is manifeft from the whole report.

Bufhel, one of the jurors on the trial of Penn and Mead, had been committed by the court for finding the defendant not guilty, againft the direction of the court in matter of law; and being brought before the court of common pleas by habeas corpus, this caufe of commitment appeared upon the face of the return to the writ. It was contended by the counfel againft Bufhel upon the authority of this maxim, that the commitment was legal, fince it appeared by the return, that Bufhel had taken upon him to find the law againft the direction of the judge, and had been therefore legally imprifoned for that contempt. It was upon that occafion that Chief Juftice Vaughan, with the concurrence of the whole court, repeated the maxim, *Ad queftionem legis non refpondent juratores*, as cited by the counfel for the crown, but denied the application of it to impofe any reftraint upon jurors

trying

trying any crime upon the general iffue. His language is too remarkable to be forgotten, and too plain to be mifunderftood. Taking the words of the return to the habeas corpus, viz. " That the " jury did acquit againft the direction of the court " in matter of law." " Thefe words (faid this' " great lawyer) taken literally and *de plano* are in- " fignificant and unintelligible, for no iffue can be " joined of matter of law, no jury can be charged " with the trial of matter of law barely: no evi- " dence ever was, or can be given to a jury of what " is law or not; nor any oath given to a jury to " try matter of law alone, nor can any attaint lie " for fuch a falfe oath. Therefore we muft take " off this veil and colour of words, which make " a fhew of being fomething, but are in fact " nothing : for if the meaning of thefe words, " *Finding againft the direction of the court in matter* " *of law,* be, that if the judge, having heard the " evidence given in court, (for he knows no other,) " fhall tell the jury upon this evidence, that the " law is for the plaintiff or the defendant, and they " under the pain of fine and imprifonment are to " find accordingly, every one fees that the jury is " but a troublefome delay, great charge, and of " no ufe in determining right and wrong; which " were a ftrange and new found conclufion, after a " trial fo celebrated for many hundreds of years in " this country."

Lord

Lord Chief Juſtice Vaughan's argument is there-fore plainly this. Adverting to the arguments of the counſel, he ſays, you talk of the maxim *Ad queſtionem legis non reſpondent juratores,* but it has no ſort of application to your ſubjeſt. The words of your return, viz. That Buſhel did acquit againſt the direction of the court in matter of law, is un-intelligible and as applied to the caſe impoſſible. The jury could not be aſked in the abſtraſt, what was the law : they could not have an iſſue of the law joined before them : they could not be ſworn to try it. *Ad queſtionem legis non reſpondent jura-tores:* therefore to ſay literally and *de plano* that the jury found the law againſt the judge's direction, is abſurd : they could not be in a ſituation to find, it ; an unmixed queſtion of law could not be be-fore them : the judge could not give any poſitive directions of law upon the trial, for the law can only ariſe out of faſts, and the judge cannot know what the faſts are till the jury have given their verdiſt. Therefore, continued the chief juſtice, let us take off this veil and colour of words, which make a ſhew of being ſomething but are in faſt nothing : let us get rid of the fallacy of applying a maxim, which truly deſcribes the juriſdiction of the courts over iſſues of law, to deſtroy the juriſ-diction of jurors, in caſes where law and faſt are blended together upon a trial. For if the jury at the trial are bound to receive the law from the judge, every one ſees that it is a mere mockery,

mockery, and of no ufe in determining right and wrong.

This is the plain common fenfe of the argument; and it is impoffible to fuggeft a diftinction between its application to Buſhel's cafe and to the prefent; except that the right of imprifoning the jurors was there contended for, in order to enforce obedience to the directions of the judge. But this diftinction, if it deferves the name, though held up by Mr. Bearcroft as very important, is a diftinction without a difference. For if, according to Vaughan, the free agency of the jury over the whole charge, un-controuled by the judge's direction, conftitutes the whole of that antient mode of trial; it fignifies nothing by what means that free agency is de-ftroyed: whether by the imprifonment of con-fcience or of body; by the operation of their vir-tues or of their fears: whether they decline exert-ing their jurifdiction from being told that the exer-tion of it is a contempt of religious and moral order, or a contempt of the court punifhable by imprifonment; their jurifdiction is equally taken away.

My Lord, I fhould be very forry improperly to wafte the time of the court, but I cannot help re-peating once again, that if in confequence of the learned judge's directions, the jury from a juft de-ference to learning and authority, from a nice and modeft fenfe of duty, felt themfelves not at liberty

M 3   to

to deliver the defendant from the whole indict-ment; he has not been tried. Becaufe though he was entitled by law to plead generally that he was not guilty; though he did in fact plead it accord-ingly and went down to trial upon it, yet the jury have not been permitted to try that iffue, but have been directed to find at all events a general verdict of guilty; with a pofitive injunction not to in-veftigate the guilt, or even to liften to any evidence of innocence.

My Lord, I cannot help contrafting this trial, with that of Colonel Gordon's but a few feffions paft in London. I had in my hand but this mo-ment, an accurate note of Mr. Baron Eyre's * charge to the jury on that occafion ; I will not detain the court by looking for it amongft my papers; be-caufe I believe I can correctly repeat the fubftance of it.

Earl of Mansfield. The cafe of the King againft Cofmo Gordon.

Mr. Erfkine. Yes, my Lord; Colonel Gordon was indicted for the murder of General Thomas, whom he had killed in a duel : and the queftion was, whether if the jury were fatisfied of that fact, the prifoner was to be convicted of murder?

That was according to Forfter as much a quef-tion of law, as libel or no libel: but Mr. Baron

* Now Lord Chief Baron.

Eyre

Eyre did not therefore feel himfelf at liberty to withdraw it from the jury. After ftating (greatly to his honour) the hard condition of the prifoner, who was brought to a trial for life, in a cafe where the pofitive law and the prevailing manners of the times were fo ftrongly in oppofition to one another, that he was afraid the punifhment of individuals would never be able to beat down an offence fo fanctioned ; he addreffed the jury nearly in thefe words : " Neverthelefs, gentlemen, I am " bound to declare to you, what the law is as ap- " plied to this cafe, in all the different views in " which it can be confidered by you upon the evi- " dence. *Of this law and of the facts as you fhall* " *find them, your verdict muft be compounded*, and I " perfuade myfelf, that it will be fuch a one as to " give fatisfaction to your own confciences."

Now, if Mr. Baron Eyre, inftead of telling the jury that a duel, however fairly and honourably fought, was a murder by the law of England, and leaving them to find a general verdict under that direction, had faid to them, that whether fuch a duel was murder or manflaughter, was a queftion with which neither he nor they had any thing to do, and on which he fhould therefore deliver no opinion ; and had directed them to find that the prifoner was guilty of killing the deceafed in a de- liberate duel, telling them, that the court would fettle the reft ; that would have been directly con- fonant to the cafe of the Dean of St. Afaph. By

M 4   this

this direction, the prifoner would have been in the hands of the court, and the judges, not the jury, would have decided upon the life of Colonel Gordon.

But the two learned judges differ moft effentially indeed.

Mr. Baron Eyre conceives himfelf bound in duty to ftate the law as applied to the particular facts, and to leave it to the jury.

Mr. Juftice Buller fays, he is not bound nor even allowed fo to ftate or apply it, and withdraws it entirely from their confideration.

Mr. Baron Eyre tells the jury that their verdict is to be compounded of the fact and the law.

Mr. Juftice Buller on the contrary, that it is to be confined to the fact only, the law being the ex-clufive province of the court.

My Lord, it is not for me to fettle differences of opinion between the judges of England, nor to pronounce which of them is wrong : but, fince they are contradictory and inconfiftent, I may hazard the affertion that they cannot both be right : the authorities which I have cited, and the general fenfe of mankind which fettles every thing elfe, muft determine the reft.

My

My Lord, I come now to a very important part of the cafe, untouched I believe before in any of the arguments on this occafion.

I mean to contend, that the learned judge's charge to the jury cannot be fupported even upon its own principles; for, fuppofing the court to be of opinion that all I have faid in oppofition to thefe principles is inconclufive, and that the queftion of libel, and the intention of the publifher were properly withdrawn from the confideration of the jury, ftill I think I can make it appear that fuch a judgment would only render the mifdirection more palpable and ftriking.

I may fafely affume, that the learned judge muft have meant to direct the jury either to find a general or a fpecial verdict ; or to fpeak more generally, that one of thefe two verdicts muft be the object of every charge : For I venture to affirm, that neither the records of the courts, the reports of their proceedings, nor the writings of lawyers, furnifh any account of a third. There can be no middle verdict between both ; the jury muft either try the whole iffue generally, or find the facts fpecially, referring the legal conclufion to the court.

I may affirm with equal certainty, that the general verdict, *ex vi termini*, is univerfally as comprehenfive as the iffue, and that confequently fuch a verdict a verdict on an indictment, upon the general iſſue, not guilty, univerſally and unavoidably involves a judgment of law, as well as fact; becauſe the charge comprehends both, and the verdict, as has been ſaid, is coextenſive with it. Both Coke and Littleton, give this preciſe definition of a general verdict; for they both ſay, that if the jury will find the law, they may do it by a general verdict, which is ever as large as the iſſue. If this be ſo, it follows by neceſſary conſequence, that if the judge means to direct the jury to find generally againſt a defendant, he muſt leave to their conſideration every thing which goes to the conſtitution of ſuch a general verdict, and is therefore bound to permit them to come to, and to direct them how to form that general concluſion from the law and the fact, which is involved in the term guilty. For it is ridiculous to ſay, that guilty is a fact, it is a concluſion in law from a fact, and therefore can have no place in a ſpecial verdict, where the legal concluſion is left to the court.

In this caſe the defendant is charged, not with having publiſhed this pamphlet, but with having publiſhed a certain falſe, ſcandalous, and ſeditious libel, with a ſeditious and rebellious intention. He pleads that he is not guilty in manner and form as he is accuſed; which plea is admitted on all hands to be a denial of the whole charge, and conſequently does not merely put in iſſue the fact of publiſhing the pamphlet; but the truth of the whole indict-

ment,

ment, *i. e.* the publication of the libel set forth in it, with the intention charged by it.

When this issue comes down for trial, the jury must either find the whole charge or a part of it ; and admitting for argument sake, that the judge has a right to dictate either of these two courses ; he is undoubtedly bound in law to make his direction to the jury conformable to the one or the other. If he means to confine the jury to the fact of publishing, considering the guilt of the defendant to be a legal conclusion for the court to draw from that fact, specially found on the record : he ought to direct the jury to find that fact without affixing the epithet of guilty to the finding. But, if he will have a general verdict of guilty, which involves a judgment of law as well as fact ; he must leave the law to the consideration of the jury. For when the word guilty is pronounced by them, it is so well understood to comprehend every thing charged by the indictment, that the associate or his clerk instantly records, that the defendant is guilty in manner and form as he is accused, *i. e.* not simply that he has published the pamphlet contained in the indictment ; but that he is guilty of publishing *the libel* with the wicked intentions charged on him by the record.

Now, if this effect of a general verdict of guilty is reflected on for a moment, the misdirection of directing one upon the bare fact of publishing, will

appear

appear in the moſt glaring colours. The learned judge ſays to the jury, Whether this be a libel is not for your conſideration ; I can give no opinion on that ſubject without injuſtice to the proſecutor ; and as to what Mr. Jones ſwore concerning the defendant's motives for the publication, that is likewiſe not before you : for, if you are ſatisfied in point of fact that the defendant publiſhed this pamphlet, you are bound to find him *guilty*. Why guilty, my lord, when the conſideration of guilt is withdrawn ? He confines the jury to the finding of a fact, and enjoins them to leave the legal con-cluſion from it to the court ; yet, inſtead of di-recting them to make that fact the ſubject of a ſpecial verdict, he deſires them in the ſame breath to find a general one : to draw the concluſion without any attention to the premiſes : to pro-nounce a verdict which upon the face of the record includes a judgment upon their oaths that the paper is a libel, and that the publiſher's intentions in publiſhing it were wicked and ſeditious, although neither the one nor the other made any part of their conſideration.

My Lord, ſuch a verdict is a monſter in law, without precedent in former times, or root in the conſtitution. If it be true, cn the principle of the charge itſelf, that the fact of publication was all that the jury were to find, and all that was ne-ceſſary to eſtabliſh the defendant's guilt, if the thing publiſhed be a libel ; Why was not that fact found

found like all other facts upon special verdicts?
Why was an epithet, which is a legal conclusion
from the fact, extorted from a jury who were re-
strained from forming it themselves? The verdict
must be taken to be general or special: if general,
it has found the whole issue without a co-exten-
five examination. If special, the word guilty
which is a conclusion from facts can have no place
in it.

Either this word guilty is operative or uneffential;
an epithet of substance, or of form. It is impossible
to controvert that proposition, and I give the
gentlemen their choice of the alternative. If they
admit it to be operative and of real substance, or,
to speak more plainly, that the fact of publication
found specially, without the epithet of guilty,
would have been an imperfect verdict inconclusive
of the defendant's guilt, and on which no judgment could have followed: then it is impossible to
deny that the defendant has suffered injustice; because such an admission confesses that a criminal
conclusion from a fact has been obtained from the
jury, without permitting them to exercise that
judgment which might have led them to a conclusion of innocence: and that the word guilty has
been obtained from them at the trial as a mere
matter of form, although the verdict without it,
stating only the fact of publication which they were
directed to find, to which they thought the finding
alone enlarged, and beyond which they never enlarged

larged their enquiry, would have been an absolute
verdict of acquittal.

If, on the other hand, to avoid this insuperable
objection to the charge, the word guilty is to be
reduced to a mere word of form, and it is to be
contended that the fact of publication found specially would have been tantamount; be it so: let
the verdict be so recorded; let the word guilty be
expunged from it, and I instantly sit down; I
trouble your Lordships no further; I withdraw my
motion for a new trial, and will maintain in arrest
of judgment, that the Dean is not convicted. But
if this is not conceded to me, and the word guilty
though argued to be but form, and though as such
obtained from the jury, is still preserved upon the
record, and made use of against the defendant as
substance; it will then become us, (independently
of all consideration as lawyers,) to consider a little
how that argument is to be made consistent with
the honour of gentlemen, or that fairness of dealing
which cannot but have place wherever justice is administered.

But in order to establish that the word guilty is
a word of essential substance; that the verdict would
have been imperfect without it; and that therefore
the defendant suffers by its insertion; I undertake
to shew your Lordship, upon every principle and
authority of law, that if the fact of publication,
which was all that was left to the jury, had been
                                                    found

found by fpecial verdict, no judgment could have
been given on it.

My Lord, I will try this by taking the fulleft
finding which the facts in evidence could poffibly
have warranted. Suppofing then, for inftance,
that the jury had found that the defendant publifhed
the paper according to the tenor of the indictment:
that it was written of and concerning the King and
his Government; and that the innuendos were
likewife as averred, K meaning the prefent King,
and P the prefent parliament of Great Britain : on
fuch a finding, no judgment could have been given
by the court, even if the record had contained a
compleat charge of a libel. No principle is more
unqueftionable than that to warrant any judgment
upon a fpecial verdict, the court which can prefume nothing that is not vifible on the record, muft
fee fufficient matter upon the face of it, which, if
taken to be true, is conclufive of the defendant's
guilt. They muft be able to fay, if this record be
true, the defendant cannot be innocent of the crime
which it charges on him. But from the facts of
fuch a verdict the court could arrive at no fuch
legitimate conclufion; for it is admitted on all
hands, and indeed exprefsly laid down by your
Lordfhip in the cafe of the King againft Woodfall,
that publication even of a libel is not *conclufive*
evidence of guilt ; for that the defendant may give
evidence of an innocent publication.

Looking

Looking therefore upon a record containing a good indictment of a libel, and a verdict finding that the defendant publifhed it; but without the epithet of guilty, the court could not pronounce that he publifhed it with the malicious intention which is the effence of the crime: they could not fay what might have paffed at the trial: for any thing that appeared to them he might have given fuch evidence of innocent motive, neceffity, or miftake, as might have amounted to excufe or juftification. They would fay that the facts ftated upon the verdict would have been fully fufficient in the abfence of a legal defence to have warranted the judge to have directed, and the jury to have given a general verdict of guilty, comprehending the intention which conftitutes the crime : but that to warrant the bench which is ignorant of every thing at the trial, to prefume that intention, and thereupon to pronounce judgment on the record, the jury muft not merely find full evidence of the crime, but fuch facts as compofe its legal definition. This wife principle is fupported by authorities which are perfectly familiar.

If, in an action of trover, the plaintiff proves property in himfelf, poffeffion in the defendant, and a demand and refufal of the thing charged to be converted; this evidence unanfwered is full proof of a converfion; and if the defendant could not fhew to the jury why he had refufed to deliver the plaintiff's

plaintiff's property on a legal demand of it, the
judge would direct them to find him guilty of the
converfion. But on the fame facts found by fpecial
· verdict, no judgment could be given by the court :
the judges would fay, If the fpecial verdict contains
the whole of the evidence given at the trial, the
jury fhould have found the defendant guilty; for
the converfion was ˙fully proved, but we cannot
declare thefe facts to amount to a converfion, for
the defendant's intention was a fact which the jury
fhould have found from the evidence, over which
we have no jurifdiction.

So in the cafe put by Lord Coke, I believe in his
firft Inftitute 115. If a modus is found to have
exifted beyond memory till within thirty years before the trial, the court cannot upon fuch facts
found by fpecial verdict pronounce againft the
modus : but any one of your Lordfhips would certainly tell the jury, that upon fuch evidence they
were warranted in finding againft it.

In all cafes of prefcription, the univerfal practice
of judges is to direct juries by analogy to the ftatute of limitations to decide againft incorporeal
rights, which for many years have been relin-
quifhed ; but fuch modern relinquifhments, if
ftated upon the record by fpecial verdict, would in
no inftance warrant a judgment againft any prefcription. The principle of the difference is obvious and univerfal : the court looking at a record

N   can

can prefume nothing; it has nothing to do with reafonable probabilities, but is to eftablifh legal certainties by its judgments. Every crime is like every other complex idea, capable of a legal definition: if all the component parts which go to its formation are put as facts upon the record, the court can pronounce the perpetrator of them a criminal: but if any of them are wanting, it is a chafm in fact, and cannot be fupplied. Wherever intention goes to the effence of the charge, it muft be found by the jury; it muft be either comprehended under the word guilty in the general verdict, or fpecifically found as a fact by the fpecial verdict. This was folemnly decided by the court in Huggins's cafe, in fecond Lord Raymond, 1581, which was a fpecial verdict of murder from the Old Bailey.

It was an indictment againft John Huggins, and James Barnes, for the murder of Edward Arne. The indictment charged that Barnes made an affault upon Edward Arne, being in the cuftody of the other prifoner Huggins, and detained him for fix weeks in a room newly built over the common fewer of the prifon, where he languifhed and died: the indictment further charged, that Barnes and Huggins well knew that the room was unwholefome and dangerous: the indictment then charged that the prifoner Huggins of his malice aforethought was prefent, aiding, and abetting Barnes,

to

to commit the murder aforefaid. This was the fubftance of the indictment.

The fpecial verdict found that Huggins was war-
den of the Fleet by letters patent: that the other
prifoner Barnes was fervant to Gibbons Huggins,
deputy in the care of all the prifoners, and of the
deceafed a prifoner there. That the prifoner Barnes,
on the 7th of September, put the deceafed Arne
in a room over the common fewer which had been
newly built, knowing it to be newly built, and
damp, and fituated as laid in the indictment: *and
that fifteen days before the prifoner's death*, HUG-
GINS *likewife well knew that the room was now built,
damp, and fituated as laid.   They found that fifteen
days before the death* of the prifoner, Huggins was
prefent in the room, and faw him there under
durefs of imprifonment, *but then and there turned
away, and Barnes locked the door, and that
from that time till his death the deceafed remained
locked up.*

It was argued before the twelve judges in Ser-
jeants Inn, whether Huggins was guilty of murder.
It was agreed that he was not anfwerable *criminally*,
for the act of his deputy, and could not be guilty,
unlefs the criminal intention was brought perfonally home to himfelf.   And it is remarkable how
ftrongly the judges required the fact of knowledge
and malice, to be ftated on the face of the verdict,

as

as oppofed to *evidence* of intention, and inference from a fact.

The court faid, it is chiefly relied on that Huggins was prefent in the room, and faw Arne *fub duritie imprifonamenti, et fe avertit ;* but he might be prefent and not know all the circumftances; the words are VIDIT *fub duritie ;* but he might *fee* him under durefs, and not *know* he was under durefs : it was anfwered that feeing him under durefs evidently means he knew he was under durefs ; but fays the court, " *we cannot take things by inference in this manner ; his feeing is but evidence of his knowledge of thefe things, and therefore the jury, if the fact would have borne it, fhould have found that Huggins knew he was there without his confent, which not being done we cannot intend thefe things nor infer them ; we muft judge of facts, and not from the evidence of facts ;*" and cited Keylnge, 78 ; that whether a man be aiding and abetting a murder is matter of fact, and ought to be exprefsly found by a jury.

The application of thefe laft principles and authorities to the cafe before the court is obvious and fimple.

The criminal intention is a fact, and muft be found by the jury : and that finding can only be exprefsed upon the record by the general verdict of guilty

guilty which comprehends it, or by the special
enumeration of such facts as do not merly amount
to evidence of, but which completely ant conclu-
sively constitute the crime. But it has been shewn,
and is indeed admitted, that the publication of a
libel is only *prima facie* evidence of the complex
charge in the indictment, and not such a fact as
amounts in itself when specially stated to conclusive
guilt; since as the judges cannot tell how the
criminal inference from the fact of publishing a
libel, might have been rebutted at the trial; no
judgment can follow from a special finding, that
the defendant published the paper indicted according to the tenor laid in the indictment.

It follows from this, that if the jury had only
found the fact of publication, which was all that
was left to them, *without affixing the epithet of guilty,*
which could be only legally affixed by an investigation not permitted to them ; a *venire facias de novo*
must have been awarded because of the uncertainty
of the verdict as to the criminal intention : whereas
it will now be argued, that if the court shall hold
the dialogue to be a libel, the defendant is fully
convicted ; because the verdict does not merely
find that he published, which is a finding confistent
with innocence, but finds him GUILTY of publishing, which is a finding of the criminal publication
charged by the indictment.

My Lord, how I shall be able to defend my innocent client against such an argument, I am not

prepared

prepared to fay; I feel all the weight of it; but that feeling furely entitles me to greater attention, when I complain of that which fubjects him to it, without the warrant of the law. It is the weight of fuchan argument that entitles me to a new trial; for the Dean of St. Afaph is not only found guilty, without any inveftigation of his guilt by the jury, but without that queftion being even open to your Lordfhips on the record. Upon the record the court can only fay the dialogue is, or is not a libel; but if it fhould pronounce it to be one, the criminal intention of the defendant in publifhing it is taken for granted by the word guilty; although it has not only not been tried, but evidently appears from the verdict itfelf not to have been found by the jury. Their verdict is, " guilty of publifhing, " but whether a libel or not they do not find." And it is therefore impoffible to fay that they can have found a criminal motive in publifhing a paper, on the criminality of which they have formed no judgment. Printing and publifhing that which is legal, contains in it no crime; the guilt muft arife from the publication of a libel; and there is therefore a palpable repugnancy on the face of the verdict itfelf, which firft finds the Dean guilty of publifhing, and then renders the finding a nullity, by pronouncing ignorance in the jury whether the the thing publifhed comprehends any guilt.

To conclude this part of the fubject, the epithet of guilty (as I fet out with at firft) muft either be taken to be fubftance, or form. If it be fubftance,

and

and as fuch, conclufive of the *criminal* intention of
the publifher, fhould the thing publifhed be hereafter adjudged to be a libel ; I afk a new trial, becaufe the defendant's guilt in that refpect has been
found without having been tried : If on the other
hand, the word GUILTY is admitted to be but a
word of form, then let it be expunged, and I am
not hurt by the verdict.

Having now eftablifhed, according to my two
firft propofitions, that the jury upon every general
iffue, joined in a criminal cafe, have a conftitutional jurifdiction over the whole charge, I am
next in fupport of my third, to contend, that the
cafe of a libel forms no legal exception to the general principles which govern the trial of all other
crimes, that the argument for the difference, viz.
becaufe the whole charge always appears on the
record, is falfe in fact, and that even if true, it
would form no fubftantial difference in law.

As to the firft, I ftill maintain that the whole
cafe does by no means neceffarily appear on the
record ; the crown may indict part of the publication, which may bear a criminal conftruction
when feparated from the context, and the context
omitted having no place in the indictment, the defendant can neither demur to it, nor arreft the judgment after a verdict of guilty; becaufe the court is
abfolutely circumfcribed by what appears on the record, and the record contains a legal charge of
a libel.

I maintain

I maintain likewife, that according to the principles adopted upon this trial, he is equally fhut
out from fuch defence before the jury; for though
he may read the explanatory context in evidence,
yet he can derive no advantage from reading it, if
they are tied down to find him guilty of publifhing
the matter which is contained in the indictment,
however its innocence may be eftablifhed by a view
of the whole work. The only operation, which
looking at the context can have upon a jury is, to
convince them that the matter upon the record,
however libellous when taken by itfelf, was not
intended to convey the meaning which the words
indicted import in language, when feparated from
the general fcope of the writing: but upon the
principle contended for, they could not acquit the
defendant upon any fuch opinion, for that would
be to take upon them the prohibited queftion of
libel, which is faid to be matter of law for the
court.

My learned friend Mr. Bearcroft appealed to
his audience with an air of triumph, whether any
fober man could believe, that an Englifh jury in
the cafe I put from Algernon Sidney would convict a defendant of publifhing the Bible, fhould
the crown indict a member of a verfe which
was blafphemous in itfelf if feparated from the
context. My Lord, if my friend had attended to
me, he would have found that in confidering fuch
fuppofition as an abfurdity, he was only repeating
my own words. I never fuppofed that a jury would
act

act so wickedly, or so absurdly, in a case where the
principle contended for by my friend Mr. Bearcroft,
carried so palpable a face of injustice, as in the instance which I selected to expose it; and which I
therefore selected to shew that there were cases in
which the supporters of the doctrine were ashamed
of it, and obliged to deny its operation: for it is
impossible to deny that if the jury can look at the
context in the case put by Sidney, and acquit the
defendant on the merits of the thing published;
they may do it in cases which will directly operate
against the principle he seems to support. This
will appear from other instances, where the injustice is equal, but not equally striking.

Suppose the crown were to select some passage
from Locke upon Government; as for instance;
" that there was no difference *between the king and*
" *the constable when either of them exceeded their*
" *authority.*" That assertion under certain circumstances if taken by itself without the context,
might be highly seditious, and the question therefore would be *quo animo* it was written: perhaps the
real meaning of the sentence might not be discover-
able by the immediate context without a view of
the whole chapter, perhaps of the whole book;
therefore to do justice to the defendant, upon the
very principle by which Mr. Bearcroft in answer-
ing Sidney's case can alone acquit the publisher of
his Bible, the jury must look into the whole Essay

on

on Government, and form a judgment of the defign of the author, and the meaning of his work.

Lord Mansfield. To be fure they may judge from the whole work.

Mr. Erfkine. And what is this, my Lord, but determing the queftion of libel which is denied to day : for if a jury may acquit the publifher of any part of Mr. Locke on Government, from a judgment arifing out of a view of the whole book, though there be no innuendos to be filled up as facts in the indictment ; what is it that bound the jury to convict the Dean of St. Afaph, as the publifher of Sir William Jones's dialogue, on the bare fact of publication, without the right of faying that his obfervations as well as Mr. Locke's, were fpeculative, abftract, and legal ?

Lord Mansfield. They certainly may in all cafes go into the whole context.

Mr. Erfkine. And why may they go into the context? clearly, my Lord, to enable them to form a correct judgment of the meaning of the part indicted, even though no particular meaning be fubmitted to them by averments in the indictment, and therefore the very permiffion to look at the context for fuch a purpofe, (where there are no innuendos to be filled up by them as facts,) is a palpable admiffion of all I am contending for, viz. the

the right of the jury to judge of the merits of the paper, and the intention of its author. *

But it is faid, that though a jury have a right to decide that a paper criminal as far as it appears on the record, is neverthelefs legal when explained by the whole work of which it is a part; yet that they fhall have no right to fay that the whole work itfelf if it happens to be all indicted, is innocent and legal. This propofition, my Lord, upon the bare ftating of it, feems too prepofterous to be ferioufly entertained; yet there is no alternative between maintaining it in its full extent, and abandoning the whole argument.

If the defendant is indicted for publifhing part of the verfe in the pfalms, " There is no God," it is afferted that the jury may look at the context, and feeing that the whole verfe did not maintain that blafphemous propofition, but only that the fool had faid fo in his heart, may acquit the defendant upon a judgment that it is no libel, to impute fuch imagination to a fool: but if the whole verfe had been indicted, viz. " the fool has faid in his heart " there is no God;" the jury on the principle contended for, would be reftrained from the fame judgment of its legality, and muft convict of blafphemy on the fact of publifhing, leaving the queftion of libel untouched on the record.

* This right was fully exercifed by the Jury who tried and acquitted Mr. Stockdale.

If

.If in the same manner, only part of this very dialogue had been indicted instead of the whole, it is said even by your Lordship, that the jury might have read the context, and then, notwithstanding the fact of publishing, might have collected from the whole, its abstract and speculative nature, and have acquitted the defendant upon that judgment of it; and yet it is contended that they have no right to form the same judgement of it upon the present occasion, although the whole be before them upon the face of the indictment; but are bound to convict the defendant upon the fact of publishing, notwithstanding they should have come to the same judgment of its legality which it is admitted they might have come to on trying an indictment for the publication of a part. Really, my Lord, the absurdities and gross departures from reason, which must be hazarded to support this doctrine are endless.

The criminality of the paper is said to be a question of law, yet the meaning of it from which alone the legal interpretation can arise, is admitted to be a question of fact. If the text be so perplexed and dubious as to require innuendos to explain, to point, and to apply obscure expression or construction, the jury alone as judges of fact, are to interpret and to say what sentiments the author must have meant to convey by his writing: yet if the writing be so plain and intelligible as to require no averments of its meaning, it then becomes so obscure

ſcure and myſterious as to be a queſtion of law, and beyond the reach of the very ſame men who but a moment before were interpreters for the judges; and though its objeɛ be moſt obviouſly peaceable and its author innocent, they are bound to ſay upon their oaths, that it is wicked and ſeditious and the publiſher of it guilty.

As a queſtion of faɛ the jury are to try the real ſenſe and conſtruɛion of the words indiɛed, by comparing them with the context; and yet if that context itſelf which affords the compariſon makes part of the indiɛtment, the whole becomes a queſtion of law; and they are then bound down to conviɛ the defendant on the faɛ of publiſhing it, without any juriſdiɛion over the meaning. To complete the juggle, the intention of the publiſher may likewiſe be ſhewn as a faɛ, by the evidence of any extrinſic circumſtances, ſuch as the context to explain the writing, or the circumſtances of miſtake or ignorance under which it was publiſhed; and yet in the ſame breath, the intention is pronounced to be an inference of law from the aɛ of publication, which the jury cannot exclude, but which muſt depend upon the future judgment of the court.

But the danger of this ſyſtem, is no leſs obvious than its abſurdity. I do not believe that its authors ever thought of infliɛing death upon Engliſhmen, without the interpoſition of a jury; yet its eſtab-

liſhment

lifhment would unqueftionably extend to annihi-
late the fubftance of that trial in every profecution
for high treafon, where the publication of any
writing was laid as the overt act. I illuftrated this
by a cafe when I moved for a rule, and called upon
my friends for an anfwer to it, but no notice has
been taken of it by any of them; this was juft
what I expected: when a convincing anfwer cannot be found to an objection, thofe who underftand controverfy never give ftrength to it by a weak
one.

I faid, and I again repeat, that if an indictment
charges that a defendant did traiteroufly intend,
compafs, and imagine the death of the king; and
in order to carry fuch treafon into execution, publifhed a paper which it fets out literatim on the face
of the record, the principle which is laid down to
day would fubject that perfon to the pains of death
by the fingle authority of the judges, without leaving any thing to the jury, but the bare fact of publifhing the paper. For, if that fact were proved,
and the defendant called no witneffes, the judge
who tried him would be warranted, nay bound in
duty by the principle in queftion, to fay to the
jury, Gentlemen, the overt act of treafon charged
upon the defendant, is the publication of this
paper, intending to compafs the death of the King;
the fact is proved, and you are therefore bound to
convict him: the treafonable intention is an inference of law from the act of publifhing; and if the
thing

thing publifhed does not upon a future examination intrinfically fupport that inference, the court will arreft the judgment, and your verdict will not affect the prifoner.

My Lord, I will reft my whole argument upon the analogy between thefe two cafes, and give up every objection to the doctrine when applied to the one, if upon the ftricteft examination it fhall not be found to apply equally to the other.

If the feditious intention be an inference of law, from the fact of publifhing the paper which this indictment charges to be a libel, is not the treafonable intention equally an inference from the fact of publifhing that paper, which the other indictment charges to be an overt act of treafon? In the one cafe as in the other, the writing or publication of a paper is the whole charge; and the fubftance of the paper fo written or publifhed makes all the difference between the two offences. If that fubftance be matter of law where it is a feditious libel, it muft be matter of law where it is an act of treafon: and if becaufe it is law the jury are excluded from judging it in the one inftance, their judgment muft fuffer an equal abridgment in the other.

The confequence is obvious. If the jury by an appeal to their confciences are to be thus limited in the free exercife of that right which was given

them

them by the conſtitution, to be a protection againſt judicial authority where the weight and majeſty of the crown is put into the ſcale againſt an obſcure individual, the freedom of the preſs is at an end : for how can it be ſaid that the preſs is free becauſe every thing may be publiſhed without a previous licence, if the publiſher of the moſt meritorious work which the united powers of genius and pa-triotiſm ever gave to the world, may be profe-cuted by information of the King's attorney general, without the conſent of the grand jury, may be convicted by the petty jury, on the mere fact of publiſhing, (who indeed without perjuring them-ſelves muſt on this ſyſtem inevitably convict him), and muſt then depend upon judges who may be the ſupporters of the very adminiſtration whoſe meaſures are queſtioned by the defendant, and who muſt therefore either give judgment againſt him or againſt themſelves.

To all this Mr. Bearcroft ſhortly anſwers, Are you not in the hands of the ſame judges, with reſ-pect to your property and even to your life, when ſpecial verdicts are found in murder, felony, and treaſon? in theſe caſes do priſoners run any hazard from the application of the law by the judges, to the facts found by the juries? Where can you poſſibly be ſafer?

My Lord, this is an argument which I can anſwer without indelicacy or offence, becauſe your Lordſhip's

fhip's mind is much too liberal to fuppofe, that I
infult the court by general obfervations on the principles of our legal government: however fafe we
might be or might think ourfelves, the conftitution never intended to inveft judges with a difcretion, which cannot be tried and meafured by the
plain and palpable ftandard of law ; and in all the
cafes put by Mr. Bearcroft, no fuch loofe difcretion
is exercifed as muft be entertained by a judgment
on a feditious libel, and therefore the cafes are
not parrallel.

On a fpecial verdiff for murder, the life of the
prifoner does not depend upon the religious, moral,
or philofophical ideas of the judges, concerning the
nature of homicide : no, precedents are fearched
for, and if he is condemned at all, he is judged
exaftly by the fame rule as others have been judged
by before him ; his conduft is brought to a precife,
clear, intelligible ftandard, and cautioufly meafured by it: it is the law therefore and not the
judge which condemns him. It is the fame in all
indiftments, or civil aftions for flander upon individuals.

Reputation is a perfonal right of the fubjeft,
indeed the moft valuable of any, and it is therefore fecured by law, and all injuries to it clearly
afcertained : whatever flander hurts a man in his
trade, fubjefts him to danger of life, liberty, or
lofs of property, or tends to render him infamous,

O   is

is the subject of an action, and in some instances
of an indictment. But in all these cases where the
malus animus is found by the jury, the judges are in
like manner a safe repository of the legal confequence; because such libels may be brought to a
well known standard of strict and positive law;
they leave no 'discretion in the judges: the determination of what words when written or spoken of
another are actionable, or the subject of an indictment, leaves no more latitude to a court sitting in
judgment on the record, than a question of title
does in a special verdict in ejectment.

.

But I beseech your Lordship, to consider by what
rule the legality or illegality of this dialogue is to
be decided by the court as a question of law upon
the record. Mr. Bearcroft has admitted in the
most unequivocal terms, (what indeed it was impossible for him to deny,) that every part of it when
viewed in the abstract was legal; but he says, there
is a great distinction to be taken between specula-
tion and exhortation, and that it is this latter which
makes it a libel. I readily accede to the truth of
the observation, but how your Lordship is to determine that difference as a question of law, is past
my comprehension: for if the dialogue in its
phrase and composition be general, and its libellous
tendency arises from the purpose of the writer, to
raise discontent by a seditious application of legal
doctrines; that purpose is surely a question of
fact if ever there was one, and must therefore be
distinctly

diſtinctly averred in the indictment, to give the cog-
,nizance of it as a fact to the jury, without which
no libel can poſſibly appear upon the record : this
is well known to be the only office of the innuendo;
becauſe the judges can preſume nothing which the
ſtricteſt rules of grammar do not warrant them to
collect intrinſically from the writing itſelf.

Circumſcribed by the record, your Lordſhip can
form no judgment of the tendency of this dialogue
to excite ſedition by any thing but the mere words:
you muſt look at it as if it was an old manuſcript
dug out of the ruins of Herculaneum; you can
collect nothing from the time when, or the circumſtances under which it was publiſhed; the
perſon by whom, and thoſe amongſt whom it was
circulated; yet theſe may render a paper at one
time, and under ſome circumſtances, dangerouſly
wicked and ſeditious, which at another time, and
under different circumſtances, might be innocent
and highly meritorious.

If puzzled by a taſk ſo inconſiſtent with the real
ſenſe and ſpirit of judicature, your Lordſhips ſhould
ſpurn the fetters of the record, and judging with
the reaſon rather than the infirmities of men, ſhould
take into your conſideration, the ſtate of men's
minds on the ſubject of equal repreſentation at this
moment, and the great diſpoſition of the preſent
times to revolution in government: if reading the
record with theſe impreſſions your Lordſhips ſhould

be

be led to a judgment not warranted by an abstract
consideration of the record, then besides that such
a judgment would be founded on facts not in evidence before the court, and not within its jurisdiction if they were; let me further remind your
Lordships, that even if those objections to the pre-
mises were removed, the conclusion would be no
conclusion of law: your decision on the subject
might be very sagacious as politicians, as moralists,
as philosophers, or as licencers of the press, but
they would have no resemblance to the judgments
of an English court of justice, because it could have
no warrant from the acts of your predecessors, nor
afford any precedent to your successors.

But all these objections are perfectly removed,
when the seditious tendency of a paper is considered as a question of fact: we are then relieved from
the absurdity of a legal discussion separated from all
the facts from which alone the law can arise; for the
jury can do what (as I observed before) your Lordships cannot do in judging by the record; they
can examine by evidence all those circumstances
that lead to establish the seditious tendency of the
paper from which the court is shut out : they may
know themselves, or it may be proved before
them, that it has excited sedition already: they
may collect from witnesses that it has been widely
circulated, and seditiously understood; or, if the
prosecution (as is wisest) precedes these conse-
sequences, and the reasoning must be a priori,
surely gentlemen living in the country are much
better

better judges than your Lordſhip, what has or has
not a tendency to diſturb the neighbourhood in
which they live, and that very neighbourhood is
the forum of criminal trial.

If they know that the ſubjeſt of the paper is the
topic that agitates the country around them ; if
they ſee danger in that agitation, and have reaſon to think that the publiſher muſt have intended
it; they ſay he is guilty. If, on the other hand,
they conſider the paper to be legal, and enlighten-
ing in principle ; likely to promote a ſpirit of aſtivity and liberty in times when the aſtivity of ſuch
a ſpirit is eſſential to the public ſafety, and have
reaſon to believe it to be written and publiſhed in
that ſpirit ; they ſay, as they ought to do, that the
writer or the publiſher is not guilty. Whereas
your Lordſhip's judgment upon the language of
the record muſt ever be in the pure abſtraſt ; ope-
rating blindly and indiſcriminately upon all times,
circumſtances, and intentions, making no diſtinc-
tion between the glorious attempts of a Sidney or a
Ruſſel, ſtruggling againſt the terrors of deſpotiſm
under the Stuarts ; and thoſe deſperate adventurers
of the year forty-five, who libelled the perſon, and
excited rebellion againſt the mild and gracious
government of our late excellent ſovereign King
George the Second.

My Lord, if the independent gentlemen of
England are thus better qualified to decide from·
cauſe of knowledge, it is no offence to the court

to

to fay, that they are full as likely to decide with impartial juftice as judges appointed by the crown. Your Lordfhips have but a life intereft in the public property, but they have an inheritance in it for their children. Their landed property depends upon the fecurity of the government, and no man who wantonly attacks it can hope or expect to efcape from the felfifh lenity of a jury. On the firft principles of human action they muft lean heavily againft him. It is only when the pride of Englifhmen is picqued by fuch doctrines as I am oppofing to-day, that they think it better to fcreen the guilty by an indifcriminate oppofition to them, than furrender thofe rights by which alone inno- cence in the day of danger can be protected.

I venture therefore to fay, in fupport of one of my original propofitions, that where a writing in- dicted as a libel, neither contains, nor is averred by the indictment to contain any flander of an in- dividual, fo as to fall within thofe rules of law which protect perfonal reputation, but whofe cri- minality is charged to confift (as in the prefent in- ftance) in its tendency to ftir up general difcontent, that the trial of fuch an indictment neither in- volves, nor can in its obvious nature involve any abftract queftion of law for the judgment of a court, but muft wholly depend upon the judgment of the jury on the tendency of the writing itfelf, to pro- duce fuch confequences, when connected with all the circumftances which attended its publication.

It

It is unneceffary to pufh this part of the argument further, becaufe I have heard nothing from the bar againft the pofition which it maintains; none of the gentlemen have, to my recolleƈtion, given the court any one fingle reafon, good or bad, why the *tendency* of a paper to ftir up difcontent, againft government, feparated from all the circumftances which are ever fhut out from the record, ought to be confidered as an abftraƈt queftion of law: they have not told us where we are to find any matter in the books to enable us to argue fuch queftions before the court; or where your Lordfhips yourfelves are to find a rule for your judgments on fuch fubjeƈts. I confefs that to me it looks more like legiflation, or arbitrary power, than Englifh judicature. If the court can fay, this is a criminal writing, *not* becaufe we know that mifchief was intended by its author, or is even contained in itfelf, but becaufe fools believing the one and the other may do mifchief in their folly; the fuppreffion of fuch writings under particular circumftances may be wife policy in a ftate, but' upon what principle it can be criminal law in England to be fettled in the abftraƈt by judges, I confefs with humility, that I have no organs to underftand.

Mr. Leycefter felt the difficulty of maintaining fuch a propofition by any argument of law, and therefore had recourfe to an argument of faƈt. " If (fays my learned friend) what is or is not a

" feditious

" feditious libel, be not a queftion of law for the
" court, but of fact for the jury, upon what prin-
" ciple do defendants found guilty of fuch libels
" by a general verdict, defeat the judgment for
" error on the record : and what is ftill more in
" point, upon what principle does Mr. Erfkine
" himfelf, if he fails in his prefent motion, mean
" to afk your Lordfhips to arreft this very judg-
" ment by faying that the dialogue is not a libel."

My Lord, the obfervation is very ingenious, and
God knows the argument requires that it fhould ;
but it is nothing more. The arreft of judgment
which follows after a verdict of guilty for publifhing
a writing, which on infpection of the record ex-
hibits to the court no fpecific offence againft the
law, is no impeachment of my doctrine : I never
denied fuch a jurifdiction to the court. My pofition is, that no man fhall be punifhed for the criminal breach of any law, until a jury of his equals
have pronounced him guilty in mind as well as in
act. *Actus non facit reum nifi mens fit rea.*

But I never afferted that a jury had the power to
make criminal law as well as to adminifter it ; and
therefore it is clear that they cannot deliver over a
man to punifhment if it appears by the record of his
accufation, which is the office of judicature to
examine, that he has not offended againft any
pofitive law ; becaufe however criminal he may
have been in his difpofition, which is a fact
                                            eftablifhed

eftablifhed by the verdict, yet ftatute and precedents can alone decide what is by law an *indictable* offence.

If, for inftance, a man were charged by an indictment with having held a difcourfe in words
highly feditious, and were found guilty by the
jury, it is evident that it is the province of the
court to arreft that judgment; becaufe though
the jury have found that he fpoke the words as laid
in the indictment, with the feditious intention
charged upon him, which· they, and they only
could find; yet as the words are not punifhable
by indictment, as when committed to writing,
the court could not pronounce judgment: the declaration of the jury that the defendant was guilty
in manner and form as accufed, could evidently
never warrant a judgment, if the accufation
itfelf contained no charge of an offence againft
the law.

In the fame manner, if a butcher were indicted
for privately putting a fheep to caufelefs and unneceffary torture in the exercife of his trade, but not
in public view fo as to be productive of evil example, and the jury fhould find him guilty, I am
afraid that no judgment could follow; becaufe
though done *malo animo*, yet neither ftatute nor
precedent have perhaps determined it to be an
indictable offence; it would be difficult to draw
the line. An indictment would not lie for every
inhuman

inhuman neglect of the fufferings of the fmalleft innocent animals which Providence has fubjected to us.

Yet the poor beetle which we tread upon,
In corporal fuffering feels a pang as great
As when a giant dies.

A thoufand other inftances might be brought of acts bafe and immoral, and prejudicial in their confequences, which are not yet indictable by law.

In the cafe of the King againft Brewer, in Cowper's reports, it was held that *knowingly* expofing to fale and felling gold under fterling for ftandard gold, is not indictable ; becaufe the act refers to goldfmiths only, and private cheating is not a common-law offence.

Here too the declaration of the jury that the defendant is guilty in manner and form as accufed, does not change the nature of the accufation : the verdict does not go beyond the charge; and if the charge be invalid in law, the verdict muft be invalid alfo.

All thefe cafes therefore, and many fimilar ones which might be put, are clearly confiftent with my principle ; I do not feek to erect jurors into legiflators or judges : there muft be a rule of action
in

in every fociety which it is the duty of the legiflature to create, and of judicature to expound when created. I only fupport their right to determine guilt or innocence where the crime charged is blended by the general iffue with the intention of the criminal; more efpecially when the quality of the act itfelf even independent of that intention, is not meafurable by any precife principle or precedent of law, but is infeparably connected with the time when, the place where, and the circumftances under which the defendant acted.

My Lord, in confidering libels of this nature as oppofed to flander on individuals to be mere queftions of fact, or at all events to contain matter fit for the determination of the jury; I am fupported not only by the general practice of courts, but even of thofe very practifers themfelves, who in profecuting for the crown have maintained the contrary doctrine.

Your Lordfhips will I am perfuaded admit that the general practice of the profeffion, more efpecially of the very heads of it, profecuting too for the public, is ftrong evidence of the law. Attorney Generals have feldom entertained fuch a jealoufy of the king's judges in ftate profecutions, as to lead them to make prefents of jurifdiction to juries, which did not belong to them of right by the conftitution of the country. Neither can it be fuppofed, that men in high office and of great experience, ſ perience, ſhould in every inſtance (though differing from each other in temper, character, and talents) uniformly fall into the ſame abſurdity of declaiming to juries upon topics totally irrelevant, when no ſuch inconſiſtency is found to disfigure the pro-feſſional conduct of the ſame men in other caſes. Yet I may appeal to your Lordſhip's recollection, without having recourſe to the ſtate trials, whether upon every proſecution for a ſeditious libel within living memory, the attorney general has not uni-formly ſtated ſuch writings at length to the jury, pointed out their ſeditious tendency which ren-dered them criminal; and exerted all his powers to convince them of their illegality, as the very point on which their verdict for the crown was to be founded.

On the trial of Mr. Horne, for publiſhing an advertiſement in favour of the widows of thoſe American ſubjects who had been *murdered* by the king's troops at Lexington; did the preſent chan-cellor, then Attorney General, content himſelf with ſaying that he had proved the publication, and that the criminal quality of the paper which raiſed the legal inference of guilt againſt the de-fendant, was matter for the court? no, my Lord, he went at great length into its dangerous and pernicious tendency, and applied himſelf with ſkill and ability to the underſtandings and the con-ſciences of the jurors. This inſtance is in itſelf deciſive of his opinion: that great magiſtrate could

not

not have acted thus upon the principle contended for to day : he never was an idle declaimer ; clofe and mafculine argument is the characteriftic of his underftanding.

The character and talents of the late Lord Chief Juftice De Grey, no lefs intitles me to infer his opinion from his uniform conduct.

In all fuch profecutions while he was in office, he held the fame language to juries, and particu- larly in the cafe of the King againft Woodfall, *(to ufe the expreffion of a celebrated writer on the oc- cafion)*, he tortured his faculties for more than two hours, to convince them that Junius's letter was a libel.

The opinions of another crown lawyer, who has fince paffed through the higheft offices of the law, and filled them with the higheft reputation, I am not driven to collect alone from his language as an Attorney General ; becaufe he carried them with him to the feat of juftice. Yet one cafe is too re- markable to be omitted.

Lord Camden profecuting Doctor Shebbeare, told the jury that he did not defire their verdict upon any other principle, than their folemn con- viction of the truth of the information, which charged the defendant with a wicked defign, to alienate

alienate the hearts of the fubjects of this country from their king upon the throne.

To compleat the account : My learned friend Mr. Bearcroft, (though laft not leaft in favour) upon this very occafion, fpoke above an hour to the jury at Shrewfbury, to convince them of the libellous tendency of the dialogue, which foon afterwards the learned judge defired them wholly to difmifs from their confideration, as matter with which they had no concern. The real fact is, that the doctrine is too abfurd to be acted upon ; too diftorted in principle, to admit of confiftency in practice : it is contraband in law, and can only be fmuggled by thofe who introduce it : it requires great talents and great addrefs to hide its deformity : in vulgar hands it becomes contemptible.

Having fupported the rights of juries, by the uniform practice of crown lawyers, let us now examine the queftion of authority, and fee how this court itfelf and its judges have acted upon trials for libels in former times ; for according to Lord Raymond in Franklin's cafe (as cited by Mr. Juftice Buller, at Shrewfbury,) the principle I am fupporting, had it feems been only broached about the year 1731, by fome men of party fpirit, and then too for the very firft time.

My

My Lord, fuch an obfervation in the mouth of
Lord Raymond, proves how dangerous it is to
take up as doctrine every thing flung out at *nifi
prius*; above all upon fubjects which engage the
paffions and interefts of government. Becaufe the
moft folemn and important trials with which
hiftory makes us acquainted; difcuffed too at the
bar of this court; and when filled with judges the
moft devoted to the crown, gives the moft decifive
contradiction to fuch an unfounded and unguarded affertion.

In the famous cafe of the feven bifhops, the queftion of libel or no libel was held unanimoufly by
the court of King's Bench trying the caufe at the
bar, to be matter for the confideration and determination of the jury; and the bifhops' petition to
the king, which was the fubject of the information, was accordingly delivered to them, when they
withdrew to confider of their verdict.

Thinking this cafe decifive, I cited it at the
trial, and the anfwer it received from Mr. Bearcroft was, that it had no relation to the point in
difpute between us, for that the bifhops were acquitted not upon the queftion of libel, but becaufe
the delivery of the petition to the king was held
to be no publication.

I was not a little furprifed at this ftate of it, but
my turn of fpeaking was then paft; fortunately to
day

day it is my privilege to fpeak laft, and I have now
lying before me the fifth volume of the ftate trials,
where the cafe of the bifhops is printed, and
where it appears that the publication was exprefsly
proved ; that nothing turned upon it in the judgment of the court; and that the charge turned
wholly upon the queftion of libel, which was exprefsly left to the jury by every one of the judges.
Lord Chief Juftice Wright, in fumming up the
evidence, told them, that a queftion had at firft
arifen about the publication, it being infifted on
that the delivery of the petition to the king had
not been proved ; that the court was of the fame
opinion, and that he was juft going to have directed them to find the bifhops not guilty, when
in came my Lord Prefident (fuch fort of witneffes
were no doubt always at hand when wanted) who
proved the delivery to his Majefty. Therefore,
continued the chief juftice, if you believe it was
the fame petition, it is a publication fufficient, and
we muft therefore come to enquire whether it be a
libel.

He then gave his reafons for thinking it within
the cafe, *de libellis famofis*, and concluded, by faying to the jury, " In fhort, I muft give you my
" ópinion : I do take it to be a libel ; if my bro-
" thers have any thing to fay to it, I fuppofe they
" will deliver their opinion." What opinion ?
not that the jury had no jurifdiction to judge of the
matter, but an opinion for the exprefs purpofe of
enabling

enabling them to give that judgment which the
law required at their hands.

Mr. Juſtice Holloway then followed the chief
juſtice, and ſo pointedly was the queſtion of libel
or no libel, and not the publication, the only
matter which remained in doubt, and which the
jury with the aſſiſtance of the court were to decide
upon; that when the learned judge went into the
faƈts which had been in evidence, the chief juſtice
ſaid to him, " Look you by the way, brother, I
" did not aſk you to ſum up the evidence, but
" only to deliver your opinion to the jury, whe-
" ther it be a libel or no." The chief juſtice's
remark, though it proves my poſition, was however very unneceſſary; for but a moment before,
Mr. Juſtice Holloway had declared he did not
think it was a libel, but addreſſing himſelf to
the jury had ſaid, " *it is left to you, gentlemen.*"

Mr. Juſtice Powell who likewiſe gave his opinion that it was no libel, ſaid *to the jury*, " But
" *the matter of it is before you, and I leave the iſſue*
" *of it to God and your own conſciences:*" And ſo
little was it in the idea of any one of the court,
that the jury ought to found their verdiƈt ſolely
upon the evidence of the publication, without attending to the criminality or innocence of the petition; that the chief juſtice himſelf conſented, on
their withdrawing from the bar, that they ſhould
carry with them all the materials for coming to

P   a judga judgment as comprehenfive as the charge; and indeed exprefsly directed that the information, the libel, the declarations under the great feal, and even the ftatute-book, fhould be delivered to them.

The happy iffue of this memorable trial, in the acquittal of the bifhops by the jury, exercifing jurifdiction over the whole charge, freely admitted to them as legal even by King James's judges, is admitted by two of the gentlemen to have prepared and forwarded the glorious æra of the revolution. Mr. Bower, in particular, fpoke with fingular enthufiafm concerning this verdict, chufing (for reafons fufficiently obvious) to afcribe it to a fpecial miracle wrought for the fafety of the nation, rather than to the right lodged in the jury to fave it by its laws and conftitution.

My learned friend finding his argument like nothing upon the earth, was obliged to afcend into heaven to fupport it : having admitted that the jury not only acted like juft men towards the bifhops, but as patriot citizens towards their country, and not being able without the furrender of his whole argument, to allow either their public fpirit, or their private juftice to have been confonant to the laws, he is driven to make them the inftruments of divine Providence to bring good out of evil, and holds them up as men infpired by God to perjure themfelves in the adminiftration

tion of juftice, in order by-the-by to defeat the effects of that wretched fyftem of judicature which he is defending to-day as the conftitution of England. For if the king's judges could have decided the petition to be a libel, the Stuarts might yet have been on the throne.

My Lord, this is the argument of a prieft, not of a lawyer; and even if faith and not law were to govern the queftion, I fhould be as far from fubfcribing to it as a religious opinion.

No man believes more firmly than I do, that God governs the whole univerfe by the gracious difpenfations of his providence, and that all the nations of the earth rife and fall at his command: but then this wonderful fyftem is carried on by the natural (though to us the often hidden) relation between effects and caufes, which wifdom adjufted from the beginning, and which fore-knowledge at the fame time rendered fufficient, without difturbing either the laws of nature or of civil fociety.

The profperity and greatnefs of empires ever depended, and ever muft depend upon the ufe their inhabitants make of their reafon in devifing wife laws, and the fpirit and virtue with which they watch over their juft execution; and it is impious to fuppofe, that men who have made no provifion for their own happinefs or fecurity in their

attention

attention to their government, are to be faved by the interpofition of heaven in turning the hearts of their tyrants to protect them.

But if every cafe in which judges have left the queftion of libel to juries in oppofition to law, is to be confidered as a miracle, England may vie with Paleftine; and Lord Chief Juftice Holt fteps next into view as an apoftle: for that great judge, in Tutchin's cafe, left the queftion of libel to the jury in the moft unambiguous terms : After fumming up the evidence of writing and publifhing, he faid to them as follows,

" You have now heard the evidence, and you
" are to confider whether Mr. Tutchin be guilty.
" They fay they are innocent papers, and no libels;
" and they fay nothing is a libel but what reflects
" upon fome particular perfon. But this is a very
" ftrange doctrine, to fay, it is not a libel re-
" flecting on the government, endeavouring to
" poffefs the people that the government is
" male-adminiftered by corrupt perfons, that are
" employed in fuch or fuch ftations either in the
" navy or army.

" To fay that corrupt officers are appointed to
" adminifter affairs, is certainly a reflection on
" the government. If people fhould not be called
" to account for poffefling the people with an ill
" opinion of the government, no government can
" fubfift.

" fubfift. For it is very neceffary for all govern-
" ments that the people fhould have a good opinion
" of it: and nothing can be worfe to any govern-
" ment, than to endeavour to procure animofities,
" as to the management of it; this has been al-
" ways looked upon as a crime, and no govern-
" ment can be fafe without it be punifhed."

Having made thefe obfervations, did the chief
juftice tell the jury that whether the publication in
queftion fell within that principle fo as to be a
libel on government, was a matter of law for the
court, with which they had no concern?—Quite
the contrary: he confidered the feditious tendency
of the paper as a queftion for their fole determination, faying to them,

" Now you are to confider, whether thefe
" words I have read to you, do not tend to beget
" an ill opinion of the adminiftration of the
" government. To tell us, that thofe that are
" employed know nothing of the matter, and
" thofe that do know are not employed. Men
" are not adapted to offices, but offices to men,
" out of a particular regard to their intereft, and
" not to their fitnefs for the places; this is the
" purport of thefe papers."

In citing the words of judges in judicature I
have a right to fuppofe their difcourfe to be perti-
nent and relevant, and that when they ftate the

P 3   defendant's

defendant's anfwer to the charge, and make re.
marks on it, they mean that the jury fhould exercife a judgment under their direction: this is the
practice we muft certainly impute to Lord Holt,
if we do him the juftice to fuppofe that he meant
to convey the fentiments which he expreffed. So
that when we came to fum up this cafe, I do not
find myfelf fo far behind the learned gentleman
even in point of exprefs authority; putting all reafon, and the analogies of law which unite to fupport me, wholly out of the queftion.

There is court of king's bench againft court of
king's bench; Chief Juftice Wright againft Chief
Juftice Lee; and Lord Holt againft Lord Raymond: as to living authorities it would be invidu-
ous to clafs them, but it is a point on which I am
fatisfied myfelf, and on which the world will be
fatisfied likewife if ever it comes to be a queftion.

But even if I fhould be miftaken in that particular, I cannot confent implicitly to receive any doctrine as the law of England, though pronounced
to be fuch by magiftrates the moft refpectable, if I
find it to be in direct violation of the very firft
principles of Englifh judicature. The great jurifdictions of the country are unalterable but by Parliament, and until they are changed by that authority, they ought to remain facred; the judges
have no power over them. What parliamentary
abridgment has been made upon the rights of
juries

juries fince the trial of the bifhops, or fince
Tutchin's cafe, when they were fully recognized
by this court? None. Lord Raymond and Lord
Chief Juftice Lee ought therefore to have looked
there to their predeceffors for the law, inftead of
fetting up a new one for their fucceffors.

But fuppofing the court fhould deny the legality
of all thefe propofitions, or admitting their legality
fhould refift the conclufions I have drawn from
them; then I have recourfe to my laft propofition,
in which I am fupported even by all thofe authorities on which the learned judge relies for the
doctrines contained in his charge; to wit,

" That in all cafes where the mifchievous inten-
" tion (which is agreed to be the effence of the
" crime) cannot be collected by fimple inference
" from the fact charged, becaufe the defendant
" goes into evidence to rebut fuch inference, the
" intention becomes then a pure unmixed queftion
" of fact, for the confideration of the jury."

I faid the authorities of the King aganift
Woodfall and Almon were with me. In the firft,
which is reported in 5th Burrow, your Lordfhip
expreffed yourfelf thus: " Where an act in itfelf
" indifferent, becomes criminal, when done with
" a particular intent, there the intent muft be
" proved and found. But where the act is itfelf
" unlawful (as in the cafe of a libel) the PROOF

" of

" of juftification or excufe, lies on the defendant;
" *and in failure thereof, the law implies a criminal*
" *intent.*" Moft luminoufly expreffed to convey
this fentiment, viz. that when a man publifhes a
libel, and has nothing to fay for himfelf, no
explanation or exculpation, a criminal intention
need not be proved : I freely admit that it need
not; it is an inference of common fenfe, not of
law. But the publication of a libel, does not ex-
clufively fhew criminal intent, but is only an
implication of law, in failure of the defendant's
proof. Your Lordfhip immediately afterwards in
the fame cafe explained this further. " There
" may be cafes where the publication may be
" juftified or excufed as lawful OR INNOCENT;
" FOR NO FACT WHICH IS NOT CRIMI-
" NAL *though the paper* BE A LIBEL can amount
" to SUCH a publication of which a defendant
" ought to be found guilty." But no queftion of
that kind arofe at the trial (i. e. on the trial of
Woodfall.) Why? Your Lordfhip immediately
explained why, " *Becaufe the defendant called no*
witneffes," exprefsly faying, that the publication
of a libel is not in itfelf a crime, unlefs the intent
be criminal. And that it is not merely in mitiga-
tion of punifhment, but that *fuch* a publication
does not warrant a verdict of guilty.

In the cafe of the King againft Almon, a magazine containing one of Junius's letters, was fold
at Almon's fhop; there was proof of that fale at
the

the trial. Mr. Almon called no witneſſes, and was found guilty. To found a motion for a new trial, an affadavit was offered from Mr. Almon, that he was not privy to the ſale, nor knew his name was inſerted as a publiſher; and that this practice of bookſellers being inſerted as publiſhers by their correſpondents without notice, was common in the trade.

Your Lordſhip ſaid, "Sale of a book in a book-
" ſeller's ſhop, is *prima facie* evidence of publica-
" tion by the maſter, and the publication of a
" libel is *prima facie* evidence of criminal intent:
" it ſtands good till anſwered by the defendant:
" it muſt ſtand till contradicted or explained,
" *and if not contradicted, explained, or exculpated,*
" BECOMES *tantamount to concluſive when the defen-*
" *dant calls no witneſſes.*"

Mr. Juſtice Aſton ſaid, " *Prima facie* evidence
" *not anſwered* is ſufficient to ground a verdict
" upon: if the defendant had a ſufficient excuſe
" he might have proved it at the trial: his having
" neglected it where there was no ſurpriſe, is no
" ground for a new one." Mr. Juſtice Willes and Mr. Juſtice Aſhhurſt agreed upon thoſe expreſs principles.

Theſe caſes declare the law beyond all contro-
verſy to be, that publication even of a libel, is no concluſive proof of guilt, but only *prima facie* evidence of it till anſwered; and that if the defendant
                                                    can

can fhew that his intention was not criminal, he
compleatly rebuts the inference arifing from the
publication ; becaufe though it remains true that
he publifhed, yet, according to your Lordfhip's exprefs words, it is not fuch a publication of which
a defendant ought to be found guilty. Apply Mr.
Juftice Buller's fumming up, to this law, and it
does not require even a legal apprehenfion to diftinguifh the repugnancy.

The advertifement was proved to convince the
jury of the Dean's motive for publifhing; Mr.
Jones's teftimony went ftrongly to it, and the
evidence to charaĉter, though not fufficient in
itfelf, was admiffible to be thrown into the fcale.
But not only no part of this was left to the jury,
but the whole of it was exprefsly removed from
their confideration, although in the cafes of
Woodfall and Almon, it was as exprefsly laid
down to be within their cognizance, and a compleat anfwer to the charge if fatisfaĉtory to the
minds of the jurors.

In fupport of the learned judge's charge, there can
be therefore but the two arguments, which I ftated
on moving for the rule : either that the defendant's
evidence, namely the advertifement; Mr. Jones's
evidence in confirmation of its being *bona fide;*
and the evidence to charaĉter, to ftrengthen that
conftruĉtion, were not fufficient proof that the
Dean believed the publication meritorious : and
publifhed it in vindication of his honeft intentions :

or

or elfe, that even admitting it to eftablifh that fact, it did not amount to fuch an exculpation as to be evidence on not guilty, fo as to warrant a verdict. I ftill give the learned judge the choice of the alternative.

As to the firft, viz. whether it fhewed honeft intention in point of fact: that was a queftion for the jury. If the learned judge had thought it was not fufficient evidence to warrant the jury's be-lieving that the Dean's motives were fuch as he had declared them; I conceive he fhould have given his opinion of it as a point of evidence, and left it there. I cannot condefcend to go further; it would be to argue a felf-evident propofition.

As to the fecond, viz. that even if the jury had believed from the evidence, that the Dean's intention was wholly innocent, it would not have warranted them in accquitting, and therefore fhould not have been left to them upon not guilty; that argument can never be fupported. For, if the jury had declared, " We find that the Dean " publifhed this pamphlet, whether a libel or not " we do not find: and we find further, that be- " lieving it in his confcience to be meritorious " and innocent, he, *bona fide*, publifhed it with " the prefixed advertifement, as a vindication of his " character from the feditious intentions, and not to " excite fedition." It is impoffible to fay, with-

out

out ridicule, that on such a special verdict the court could have pronounced a criminal judgment.

Then why was the consideration of that evidence, by which those facts might have been found, withdrawn from the jury, after they brought in a verdict guilty of publishing ONLY, which in the King against Woodfall, was only said not to negative the criminal intention, because the defendant called no witnesses? Why did the learned judge confine his enquiries to the innuendos, and finding them agreed in, direct the epithet of guilty, without asking the jury if they believed the defendant's evidence to rebut the criminal inference? Some of them positively meant to negative the criminal inference, by adding the word only, and all would have done it, if they had thought themselves at liberty to enter upon that evidence. But they were told expressly that they had nothing to do with the consideration of that evidence, which, if believed, would have warranted that verdict. The conclusion is evident; if they had a right to consider it, and their consideration might have produced such a verdict, and if such a verdict would have been an acquittal, it must be a misdirection.

" But," says Mr. Bower, " if this advertisement " prefixed to the publication, by which the Dean
" professed

" profeffed his innocent intention in publifhing it
" fhould have been left to the jury as evidence of
" that intention, to found an acquittal on, even
" taking the dialogue to be a libel; no man could
" ever be convicted of publifhing any thing how-
" ever dangerous: for he would only have to tack
" an advertifement to it by way of preface, pro-
" feffing the excellence of its principles and the
" fincerity of his motives, and his defence would
" be compleat."

My Lord, I never contended for any fuch pofition.
If a man of education, like the Dean, were to
publifh a writing fo palpably libellous, that no
ignorance or mifapprehenfion imputable to fuch
a perfon could prevent his difcovering the mifchievous defign of the author; no jury would believe fuch an advertifement to be *bona fide*, and
would therefore be bound in confcience to reject it,
as if it had no exiftence: the effect of fuch evidence
muft be to convince the jury of the defendant's
purity of mind, and muft therefore depend upon
the nature of the writing itfelf, and all the circumftances attending its publication.

If upon reading the paper and confidering the
whole of the evidence, they have reafon to think
that the defendant did not believe it to be illegal,
and did not publifh it with the feditious purpofe
charged by the indictment; he is not guilty upon
any principle or authority of law, and would have
been

been acquitted even in the ftar-chamber : for it was held by that court in Lambe's cafe, in the eighth year of King James the Firft, as reported by Lord Coke who then prefided in it; that every one who fhould be convicted of a libel, muft be the writer or contriver, or a *malicious* publifher *knowing* it to be a libel.

This cafe of Lambe being of too high authority to be oppofed, and too much in point to be paffed over: Mr. Bower endeavours to avoid its force by giving it a new conftruction of his own: he fays, that not knowing a writing to be a libel, in the fenfe of that cafe, means, not knowing the contents of the thing publifhed; as by conveying papers fealed up, or having a fermon and a libel, and delivering one by miftake for the other. In fuch cafes he fays, *ignorantia facti excufat*, becaufe the mind does not go with the act; *fed ignorantia legis non excufat;* and therefore if the party knows the contents of the paper which he publifhes, his mind goes with the act of publication, tho' he does not find out any thing criminal, and he is bound to abide by the legal confequences.

This is to make criminality depend upon the confcioufnefs of an act, and not upon the know-ledge of its quality, which would involve lunatics and children in all the penalties of criminal law : for whatever they do is attended with confcioufnefs though their underftanding does not reach to the confcioufnefs of offence.

The

The publication of a libel, not believing it to be one after having read it, is a much more favourable cafe than publifhing it unread by miftake; the one, nine times in ten is a culpable negligence which is no excufe at all; for a man cannot throw papers about the world without reading them, and afterwards fay he did not know their contents were criminal: but if a man reads a paper, and not believing it to contain any thing feditious, having collected nothing of that tendency himfelf; publifhes it among his neighbours as an innocent and ufeful work, he cannot be convicted as a criminal publifher. How he is to convince the jury that his purpofe was innocent, though the thing publifhed be a libel, muft depend upon circumftances; and thefe circumftances he may on the authority of all the cafes antient and modern, lay before the jury in evidence; becaufe if he can eftablifh the innocence of his mind, he negatives the very gift of the indictment.

" In all crimes," fays Lord Hale in his pleas of the crown, " the intention is the principal confi-
" deration: it is the mind that makes the taking
" of another's goods to be felony, or a bare
" trefpafs only: it is impoffible to prefcribe all the
" circumftances evidencing a felonious intent, or
" the contrary; but the fame muft be left to the
" attentive confideration of judge *and jury;*
" wherein the beft rule is in dubiis, rather to
" incline to acquittal than conviction."

In

In the same work he says, " By the statute of
" Philip and Mary, touching importation of coin,
" counterfeit of foreign money, it must to make
" it treason, be the intent to utter and make pay-
" ment of the same; and the intent in this case
" may be tried and found by circumstances of
" FACT, by words, letters, and a thousand evi-
" dences besides the bare doing of the fact."

This principle is illustrated by frequent practice,
where the intention is found by the jury as a fact
in a special verdict.

It occurred not above a year ago, at East Grin-
stead, on an indictment for burglary, before Mr.
Justice Ashurst, where I was myself counsel for the
prisoner. It was clear upon the evidence that he
had broken into the house by force in the night,
but I contended that it appeared from proof, that
he had broken and entered with an intent to rescue
his goods, which had been seized that day by the
officers of excise; which rescue though a capital
felony by modern statute, was but a trespass, temp.
Henry VIII. and consequently not a burglary.

Mr. Justice Ashurst saved this point of law,
which the twelve judges afterwards determined for
the prisoner; but in order to create the point of
law, it was necessary that the prisoner's intention
should be ascertained as a fact; and for this purpose, the learned judge directed the jury to tell
him

him with what intention, they found that the prifoner broke and entered the houfe, which they did by anfwering, " To refcue his goods ;" which verdict was recorded.

In the fame manner in the cafe of the King againft Pierce, at the Old Bailey, the intention was found by the jury as a fact in the fpecial verdict. The prifoner having hired a horfe and afterwards fold him, was indicted for felony; but the judges doubting whether it was more than a fraud, unlefs he originally hired him intending to fell him, recommended it to the jury to find a fpecial verdict, comprehending their judgment of his intention, from the evidence. Here the quality of the act depended on the intention, which intention it was held to be the exclufive province of the jury to determine, before the judges could give the act any legal denomination.

My Lord, I am afhamed to have cited fo many authorities to eftablifh the firft elements of the law, but it has been my fate to find them difputed. The whole miftake arifes from confounding criminal with civil cafes. If a printer's fervant, without his mafter's confent or privity, inferts a flanderous article againft me in his newfpaper, I ought not in juftice to indict him; and if I do, the jury *on fuch proof* fhould acquit him; but it is no defence to an action, for he is refponfible to me civiliter for the damage which I have fuftained from

Q   the

the newfpaper, which is his property. Is there
any thing new in this principle? fo far from it
that every ftudent knows it as applicable to all
other cafes; but people are refolved from fome
fatality or other, to diftort every principle of law
into nonfenfe, when they come to apply them to
printing; as if none of the rules and maxims
which regulate all the tranfactions of fociety had
any reference to it.

If a man rifing in his fleep, walks into a china
fhop, and breaks every thing about him; his being afleep is a compleat anfwer to an indictment
for a trefpafs, but he muft anfwer in an action
for every thing he has broken.

If the proprietor of the York coach, though
afleep in his bed at that city, has a drunken fervant on the box at London, who drives over my
leg and breaks it, he is refponfible to me in da-
mages for the accident; but I cannot indict him
as the criminal author of my misfortune. What
diftinction can be more obvious and fimple.

Let us only then extend thefe principles, which
were never difputed in other criminal cafes, to the
crime of publifhing a libel; and let us at the fame
time allow to the jury as our forefathers did before us, the fame jurifdiction in that inftance,
which we agree in rejoicing to allow them in all
others, and the fyftem of Englifh law will be wife,
harmonious, and compleat.

My

My Lord, I have now finifhed my argument, having anfwered the feveral objections to my five original propofitions, and eftablifhed them by all the principles and authorities which appear to me to apply, or to be neceffary for their fupport. In this procefs I have been unavoidably led into a length not more inconvenient to the court than to myfelf, and have been obliged to queftion feveral judgments which had been before queftioned and confirmed.

They however who may be difpofed to cenfure me for the zeal which has animated me in this caufe, will at leaft, I hope, have the candour to give me credit for the fincerity of my intentions: it is furely not my intereft to ftir oppofition to the decided authorities of the court in which I practice: with a feat here within the bar, at my time of life, and looking no farther than myfelf, I fhould have been contented with the law as I found it, and have confidered *how little* might be faid with decency, rather than *how much*; but feeling as I have ever done upon the fubject, it was impoffible I fhould act otherwife. It was the firft command and council to my youth, always to do what my confcience told me to be my duty, and to leave the confequences to God. I fhall carry with me the memory, and I hope, the practice of this parental leffon to the grave: I have hitherto followed it, and have no reafon to complain that the adherence to it has been even a tem-

poral

poral facrifice; I have found it on the contrary,
the road to profperity and wealth, and fhall
point it out as fuch to my children. It is impoffible in this country to hurt an honeft man;
but even if it were, I fhould little deferve that
title, if I could upon any principle have con-
fented to tamper or temporife with a queftion
which involves in its determination and its confequences, the liberty of the prefs; and in that
liberty, the very exiftence of every part of the
public freedom.

www.ingramcontent.com/pod-product-compliance
Lightning Source LLC
Chambersburg PA
CBHW030406270326
41926CB00009B/1291